Learning How To Be A Parent

Has Taught Me How to Be . . .

A ROYAL CHILD

by
Cheryl Salem

God bless you!
Love,
Cheryl Salem

Harrison House
Tulsa, Oklahoma

Learning How To Be A Parent
Has Taught Me How To Be... A Royal Child
ISBN 0-89274-931-8
Copyright © 1995 by Cheryl Salem
P. O. Box 701287
Tulsa, Oklahoma 74170

Published by Harrison House, Inc.
P. O. Box 35035
Tulsa, Oklahoma 74153

Table of Contents

Dedication

I would like to dedicate this book to my precious husband, Harry, and our children, Lil' Harry, Roman, and Gabrielle. Without their love and support I know I would have never found the depth of healing and restoration that has been afforded me.

Praise God for strong people like you, Harry, who are willing to tell me the truth about myself and help me discover how to be completely free. Proverbs 27:17 says, "Iron sharpens iron." I know that you and I are both iron, and at times we feel like clashing swords! But in the process of working out our differences, you have never allowed me to stay the same. You have continually challenged me to be better, stronger, and wiser.

Harry, since we met I have always said that if two people agree on everything, then one of them is completely unnecessary! I know this is true. Thank you for loving me enough to challenge me to be all God has created me to be and never to accept anything less! I love you.

Foreword

Before you read the first page of this book, close your eyes and imagine a dusty old country road on a hot summer day. This peaceful scene is suddenly shattered as cars collide and tragedy strikes a little eleven-year-old girl. She wakes up in the hospital in a full body cast, crippled for life, with no way out.

Now envision an old revival meeting in the South on a hot summer night. A "faith healer" has come to town, and that same crippled girl, now a teenager, catches a ride to this meeting. With only her Bible and her simple faith, by the end of the evening she walks out of the church completely whole.

Years later, now a young woman, that same country girl is in Atlantic City, competing with the most beautiful women in the United States for the crown of Miss America. In the twinkling of an eye, like a shooting star, the dream she has carried in her heart since childhood becomes reality: She becomes Miss America.

But Cheryl never stood in the winners' circle for herself, for she knew she was there only by the faithfulness and grace of the One who had never left her or forsaken her. She simply gave thanks to Him, Who made it all possible: her personal Lord and Savior Jesus Christ.

But none of these things move me, neither count I my life dear unto myself, so that I might finish my course with joy, and the ministry, which I have received of the Lord Jesus, to testify the gospel of the grace of God.

Acts 20:24

7

When Cheryl was crowned Miss America, she was then as she is now: a true winner with the heart of a champion. Overcoming obstacles by her faith and trust in God has been the norm in this beautiful lady's life. She stared death in the face and overcame tragedy at a very early age, but she still had many battles ahead.

The doctors told her she would never walk or have children, but she has done both. In my estimation, no woman walked that prestigious walkway in Atlantic City more graciously than she did, and she is now the mother of three, raising them with the same faith and love for God.

In this book, Cheryl will become a close friend to you, maybe as close as a family member. She will encourage you through her wit, knowledge of the Bible, and pure strength in difficult circumstances. Her courage will inspire you. Begin to believe for your dreams for your life and family. Release your faith so God may reveal Himself to you and show Himself strong in the same way He has for her. You are also a Royal Child!

Harry Salem II

1
Harry Salem:
The Beginning of Restoration

There comes a moment in every person's life when destiny takes over and your life is never the same. That moment was tapping me on the shoulder, but I was totally unaware of it.

It all started when I agreed to be a guest on Richard Roberts' national television program. As I flew to Tulsa a few weeks later, little did I know I was walking straight into God's divine plan for my life.

I was picked up at the airport and rushed to the studio just in time to rehearse with the audio equipment and cameras. The rehearsal went well, and I got a chance to meet Lindsay and Richard Roberts and go over the format. Also, I met Lindsay's mother, an extremely nice and friendly woman.

During the show, I noticed a very nice looking young man standing over to the side of the set with a very serious look on his face. I assumed that he was deep in thought and must be a director or producer. The show went well and I felt very good about it.

After we went off the air, Lindsay leaned over to me and said, "Have you met the producer of the show?" When I told her that I had not, she pointed to the man whom I had noticed earlier. I said, "Oh, him," and she laughed. I figured that every time she pointed him out she must have gotten that same kind of reaction.

I was due to speak to the Oral Roberts University students in a chapel service momentarily, so we were not introduced at that moment. I spoke and sang in the chapel service and afterwards was escorted off to a waiting room in the back of the chapel to meet again with Richard and Lindsay. As I was entering the room Richard took me by the arm and said a friend of his asked if he could talk to me. To my surprise it was the mysterious producer.

Harry Salem introduced himself to me and said in all the years that he had been at ORU he had never asked Richard for a favor. But he had asked Richard if he could arrange two minutes with me.

Well, of course, I was flattered. He promptly knocked the wind out of that flattery, though, when he began to talk to me. He said that he was present at the chapel service and knew that everyone had enjoyed it. Further, he had seen me as a strong and powerful vessel of the Lord. But he had also seen something else: a hurting, troubled person beneath that strong exterior.

That was all it took! He had no idea that I was being pursued by a stalker who had been harassing me for weeks on end. I spilled my guts to him. I told him all my fears about being stalked, my security problems, and everything else I could think of! He asked if there was anything he could do and said he had some friends that might be able to help me. He gave me his phone number and said to call him if I had any questions or if I needed anything.

You won't believe this! I LOST THE NUMBER! But his advice had been helpful. Eventually, the stalker stopped and my life began to get back in order.

The next month I was contacted again to be on the show, and I flew to Tulsa. I was secretly hoping to get to see Harry again. I saw him off to the side of the set during the show but didn't get a chance to talk to him.

The guest coordinator, who had been assigned to take care of me this trip, asked if my traveling companion and I would like to have lunch. When we went into the restaurant, Harry was there having lunch with some of the crew from the show. I asked him if he would join us.

I was delighted to get to see him and talk to him. He was not the mysterious character I had thought in the beginning. He was fun, light-hearted, and very handsome. But he didn't act very interested in me. I found out he was seeing someone. And that was fine with me. I already had decided I would probably be alone the rest of my life to fulfill the call of God in my life.

That night Richard and Lindsay took me to dinner and asked if I would consider becoming a regular on the television program. They had a local pastor co-hosting with them and felt that a female singer would be a positive addition to the television family.

Their offer was very tempting to me, so we discussed my traveling schedule. They said it didn't matter if I was gone some of the time, so long as I would be on the show when I was in town. This was an answered prayer. I told them I wanted to try it on a trial basis and see if it would work for both of us.

I went back to Nashville, told my staff my decision, packed a very full bag and moved to Tulsa. I moved into an apartment and settled into a new life. During this time I came to realize what a great opportunity this was for me in Tulsa.

The Roberts' family was extremely loving and caring. I immediately fell in love with Lindsay. She was the friend I needed so desperately. She spent time with me, listened to me, didn't care that I was a former Miss America and just let me be me. She made me feel so comfortable and loved. Richard treated me like a little sister, very protective and supportive of my ministry. I very quickly decided I wanted to be a part of this ministry team.

Lindsay and Richard had overcome so many obstacles in their own marriage, some because of outside comments from not-so-well-meaning people. And they had to deal with the loss of their first born son, Richard Oral. I couldn't understand how anyone could survive such heartbreak. But their strength made me realize once again that winners can survive anything. They reminded me of that fact just by being with them.

The Roberts family gave me much strength, but had no idea they were doing it! I guess that's what made me realize I was going to be all right, that I was going to overcome the heartaches I had experienced in my own life. Thank God for the Roberts family!

Prior to this time, right after my Miss America year, Oral Roberts had written and asked me to be a part of his ministry. Even though I wanted desperately to be a part, I just couldn't seem to find peace about it. Now I know Oral was right all along. It was the *timing* that I had to wait on to be correct. Here I was in a test to see if I was going to fit into their ministry and I couldn't see myself ever leaving! Thank God for His perfect timing.

I knew God had brought me here to be a help to them on television and to be a help to Lindsay, as well. I had no idea God was going to use this place to heal some of my deepest wounds and give me back a part of my life which I thought I had lost forever!

After moving into my apartment and getting comfortable, I started doing the show and began spending more time around the television staff. Yet I still hadn't had the opportunity to talk with Harry again. Even though he was seeing someone else, I thought he might be interested in the outcome of the problem he had helped me with.

Toward the end of the week he did call me. I was delighted to see him, and we had a wonderful talk.

In the course of the conversation, Harry said how much he objected to women wearing lipstick, which came from boyhood memories of his Lebanese aunts. They would hug him, pinch his cheeks, and kiss him, leaving greasy, bright red lipstick all over his face. I quietly got up and went into the kitchen, got a paper towel (pretty hard on the lips but speed was of the essence here!), and wiped my lipstick off. I came back in the room and sat down on my end of the couch.

Nothing was said of this gesture, but I was sure that he had not missed my intent. Harry told me later *that* was the moment when he decided that he was going to marry me. It wasn't that he was opposed to lipstick, but he was testing me to see how much of my comfort zone I was willing to give up to make him happy. Make-up was definitely my comfort zone!

One year later, with the biggest grin on his face, Harry handed me the most valuable tube of lipstick I have ever owned. "You have made your point," he smiled. The subject has never been mentioned since — but I have to admit that I am very careful to avoid wearing bright red lipstick, however!

Harry's sudden realization that he was going to marry me came as quite a shock to him, because he thought he would never find the right person. We talked for a little while longer, and nothing was ever said about our feelings for each other, but we both knew our lives were changing with every word we spoke.

Harry said he had to break off a relationship with someone else, and could not pursue our relationship until he did. He didn't touch me, hug me, or kiss me. I could tell he wanted to, but he wouldn't because of this other lady in his life. That was when I decided I was going to marry him. I had never met anyone so loyal, and I certainly needed that kind of loyalty in my life.

The next week Harry and I found ourselves traveling and working in the same city, so he met me at the airport to take me to dinner. A few miles down the road he pulled the car over and promptly told me that he wanted to marry me. It was not in the form of a question, more of a statement. I was not sure how to respond since it was not a question, so I just said, "OK". What else was there to say! By the way, after he asked me to marry him he finally kissed me!

I went back on the road traveling and ministering, so we didn't see each other very much for the next few weeks. When I finally got back to Tulsa, his mother, Patricia, asked me if I would be more comfortable moving in with her since she was a widow and lived by herself. I was so thankful for the opportunity to get to know her. I fell in love with her. She and I developed a deep and lasting friendship over the next few weeks. She is a precious woman, and I knew that she would make the most wonderful mother-in-law. (She has never disappointed me!)

Harry and I were spending so little time together that we were beginning to wonder if we would ever see each other. He finally told me that if we didn't get our calendars together and come up with a date to get married, it might not ever happen! We decided on the only open weekend that both of us had for months. We ran off and got married. No one knew where we were or what we were up to and we didn't bother to tell them. I think we both needed to know that we had heard from God and that we were going to follow His direction.

Many times I look back on those months and realize that we weren't in love. We really weren't even friends yet because love and friendship come with time and getting to know each other. We were in the "know." What I mean by that is we both knew that God had spoken to us and that we weren't going to miss Him. We both knew that love is a choice, not a feeling, and we had already made that choice. I thank God that this decision was made in our spirits and our minds, and that it was not a result of emotions.

This is where many people make a grave mistake. Falling in love comes with time. Heartfelt, and sometimes painful, choices have to be made in order to stick with the leading of the Lord — regardless of the circumstances. This is what we had done and we didn't need or want a lot of other people's opinions at that point.

We came back and told his mother, but no one else. Patricia told me God had already spoken to her and told her I was to be her daughter-in-law. Isn't God wonderful? If we would just learn to trust Him and listen to the voice of the Holy Spirit then we sure would be more prepared for our future!

A few months later we went on a working vacation. (That seems to be the only kind people get today.) I noticed I was not feeling well, but I thought it was from the exhaustion of traveling and ministering. By the second week I began to realize I was over a week late. I felt different than I had ever felt before, so I took a pregnancy test. Guess what? It was positive!

Harry was white as a sheet when I told him. In fact, he made me go back and get another test and take it again! That test was positive, also! I was shocked at the news too, mostly because I had been told that I might not be able to have children. No matter how surprised we were, we were so thrilled we could hardly speak!

Harry was immediately sure our baby was a boy. He said he believed that God was giving him back something the devil had stolen from him when he was a little boy, a father-son relationship. You see, when he was only nine years old, his daddy became sick and died. Harry missed those years of spending time with his father. Doing those things that fathers and sons do together was very important to him and had been a desire of his heart for a very long time. When he realized that I was pregnant he knew God was honoring the desire of his heart (Psalm 37:4). He was going to get that father-son relationship back.

Over the next few months we had some very difficult mountains to overcome. I have always been a very independent person, doing what God had called me to do. I had married a man who wanted a wife he could see more than a few hours a week.

That was not the only struggle. Harry wanted me to call him when I traveled to let him know I had arrived safely. I knew in my heart this was a reasonable request, yet for some reason I just couldn't remember to do it every time. I realize now that part of me was rebelling against submission (See Ephesians, chapter 5) because I didn't want to be dependent on Harry emotionally.

Another part of me just got caught up in the excitement and busyness of traveling, ministering, and being with people. When my wife/mother hat would come off and my traveling minister hat would go on, I would really forget to call — but it was also more convenient to forget.

It was just easier not to call, because when I heard Harry's voice, not only would I miss him, but I knew I was causing him pain by my being away, and I would feel guilty. So, it just seemed easier to forget to call. Easier for me, maybe, but not for Harry! I have learned a lot about thinking of Harry's feelings before my own over the years, but I sure didn't start out that way!

It got to the point that every trip I took seemed to include a disagreement with Harry on the phone. Because I was being so stubborn about not submitting to his request to call him, our relationship was really being strained. It wasn't like he was asking me to stop traveling and ministering. He just wanted me to include him in my life even when we were apart. It seems so simple now, but at the time it was not clear at all!

Harry would have liked me to stay home all the time and give up the ministry, but the Lord had taken care of that. I had reached the point where I told the Lord that if something did not change in our relationship, I was going to have to come off the road. I felt my traveling was hurting our marriage, and I knew that wasn't His will! I didn't talk it over with Harry; I just told the Lord.

One day Harry attended a crusade. As the speaker was ministering, the Lord spoke very plainly to Harry. "You have your ministry and work, and Cheryl supports you in it. I have called her to her ministry, and you must support her in it. For I have truly called her at this time. If you stand between her and her calling, you will soon stand before Me."

Harry said he had never heard anything like that before, but he knew it was God. He told me later he wasn't sure if he had heard an audible voice, but that was certainly the impression he had. He said he wasn't certain if God meant He was going to visit him or he was going to be taken to heaven — either way, he didn't want to find out! He knew I had a calling on my life and I had to fulfill it. There was no doubt in his mind, and he was not going to be the one held accountable if I did not fulfill that calling. Isn't God wonderful?

When I told God my need for Harry to understand the call on my life, He spoke to Harry about it. He will help us to do His will. And if we are missing His will, He will tell us. It was God's will for me to continue ministering and for Harry to understand that. But I have to say that all this hinged on the fact that Harry was willing to truly open himself up before the Lord.

This was only one of many instances where God has used and continues to use my husband Harry to protect me, strengthen me, restore me, and make me whole.

I grew up in a family where everyone had one focus — singing gospel music — and we were constantly together. In Choctaw County, Mississippi, eight miles from the nearest town of 2,000 people, my friends were my siblings. My family sang, traveled, and ministered the gospel all over the South, from the time I was five years old until I was twenty-two years old.

When I was eleven years old my two brothers, my sister, and myself were in a terrible car accident. This tragedy left scars all over my face, my left leg crushed, and my back cracked. I was told by doctors that I would probably never walk again, but I believed God would heal me and He did. However, I still have scars to remind me of what God has brought me through.

Another "dark" side to my growing up was that I was sexually abused as a child. That part of my life was a big secret from all others, and as a result of it, I spent my life trying to be good enough, pure enough, clean enough, and deserving enough to receive approval from everyone around me. As I matured, I began to enter beauty pageants. Not only did this bring me approval, but it was a way of establishing a small amount of emotional independence apart from my family.

My perception of my worth was so warped from the abusive lies of the devil that I could never measure up in my own eyes. Even finally winning the Miss America Pageant in 1980 wasn't good enough, and my lack of self-esteem caused me to marry for all the wrong reasons.

After my year as Miss America I married a family friend. I just knew this marriage would make me feel accepted. What a mistake! My marriage didn't fill the void inside me. Four years later, as my marriage was coming to an end, I finally began to let the Lord heal me of my emotional and mental scars.

Still, the marriage ended, and once again I felt all the old shame, unworthiness, and failure. I thought divorce was what I deserved. Somewhere in the tormented thoughts of a little sexually abused girl I thought I had caused myself all these problems and an unsuccessful marriage was God's punishment to me because I was dirty and guilty.

The irony of all this was that I was preaching, singing, and believing that God is a good God! But in one little dark secret place of my emotions, I really believed God was allowing this failure in marriage because the sexual abuse was all my fault!

Now I realize how ridiculous this thinking was, but then I had not broken the curse of abuse and did not know how to silence the lies of the enemy. The demonic spirit of abuse was still tormenting me in my thought life.

When I went to Oral Roberts University to do Richard and Lindsay's television show, I was broken, wounded, and battered emotionally. Now you can understand why it touched me so deeply when God told Harry that I was being stalked and then used him to set me free of that torment. I thought I was just taking a very kind man's advice, but it was really the beginning of trusting a man to protect me and watch over me.

God put a man in my life who, through many years of chipping away at my layers of hurt and childish misunderstanding, helped me find the healing, the hope, and the restoration I so desperately needed. Harry Salem was the beginning of restoration in my life!

2
Little Harry: Strength

To think that you will never have children is a devastating thought if you are a young woman. So to be pregnant when you have thought for years that you might not ever be able to have children is extremely exhilarating! Harry and I both knew that God was shining down His favor upon us.

Early in my walk with the Lord I learned how to rely on His strength and draw from Him. I became a warrior before I ever became pregnant. So when Harry and I faced the enemy head on with our first pregnancy we began to bond together with our faith. Neither of us was willing to give the enemy an inch. Having children was vitally important to both of us, so our commitment to each other and to the Lord became stronger than ever.

We were somewhat careful about my work schedule in the beginning, but it didn't take long to realize I was going to be a very healthy pregnant woman. I felt good.

I was a little concerned about gaining too much weight so I was careful about what I ate. I followed the instructions exactly on what the doctor recommended for caloric intake for my size, height, and age. I stuck right to the program and exercised almost every day until the very end of the pregnancy. I only gained twenty pounds and felt great.

Harry was very attentive during the pregnancy. He would bring me my nightly requests for cravings and asked very little of me for the duration of the pregnancy. That was a real blessing. It gave me the opportunity to spend quiet time before the Lord and to get comfortable with the changes going on in my body, mind, and spirit. This is very important to a pregnant woman.

I truly believe if this atmosphere were available to every woman, especially during her first pregnancy, there would be far less postpartum blues. The emotional changes and hormonal changes are also much more tolerable when you have a positive attitude and when you choose to be happy.

I had no idea what labor and delivery would be like. On March twentieth at 3:00 a.m. I woke up knowing I was in labor. I wasn't really experiencing pain. It was more a feeling of excitement about the unknown, of defeating Satan once again in another area of my life, and giving Harry a son.

By 7:00 a.m. Harry and I were timing the contractions regularly so we called the doctor. He told us to come in to check my progress and to confirm that I truly was in labor.

I was in labor but moving at a snail's pace! The doctor sent me back home to labor where I was more comfortable and to walk. I must have walked forty miles that day in a circle in our dining room!

I thought, *This isn't so bad. If this is as bad as it gets this won't be anything too hard to handle. I can have a hundred children if this is all there is to it!* Boy, did I have a lot to learn in the next twenty-four hours!

By that evening the contractions were much more intense and I was beginning to tire out. I had been so excited all day that I had not rested! I had walked and walked and walked, never realizing I was going to need some strength later to finish what we had started!

At 10:00 p.m. Harry took me to the hospital to stay. After laboring all day long I still was accomplishing very little! This was disheartening but I tried to keep my faith high and my confession positive regardless of my slow progress. All night long I sat in a rocking chair breathing and focusing and having one contraction after another.

By 7:00 a.m. on the twenty-first I was exhausted. I had been at this laboring stuff for twenty-eight hours and very little was happening! I was tired, sick to my stomach, and getting a little edgy about the delivery! The doctor broke my water, I threw up, and things finally began to progress — or that's what we thought.

My body began responding to the intense contractions and started opening up. I started pushing at 11:25 a.m. with great expectation that this was soon to be over. Normally a woman pushes for an average of thirty minutes to an hour. So when an hour passed and I still didn't have a baby and it didn't look like we were any closer, I was getting pretty fed up with the whole situation.

My friend and coach, Denise, wouldn't let me feel sorry for myself. She kept reminding me I didn't have enough energy to waste on unnecessary emotions like whining and complaining. She kept me focused on the job I had to complete, telling me this was not the time to give up, and that there was no going back at this point anyway! This was a very good word for me. Give me a goal and I can complete it!

Did you wonder where Harry was all this time? He was right there with me, sitting beside me in a chair, turning green from watching me in pain, not at all sure this was the natural progression of things. I have heard so many women talk about getting angry at their husbands while they were in labor, but Harry's face was so full of sympathy, I really couldn't have been upset with him. He was wonderful, quiet, and supportive. I felt more sorry for Harry than I did for myself. He looked pitiful and precious all at the same time!

By 1:55 p.m., almost thirty-six hours after my labor had begun, little Harry Assad Salem III arrived on the scene. He was eight pounds three ounces, twenty and a half inches long, with a fourteen and a half inch head and a fourteen and a half inch chest (without measuring the arms)! What a big boy!

I couldn't quite figure out why his little head was pointed on the top until the doctor explained why the delivery had taken so long. Little Harry had gotten lodged behind my tail bone and couldn't get out. That's why I pushed so long and nothing was happening. There had come a point when the doctor had to make an incision, push the baby back up the canal, and hold my tail bone down. That's when the baby came! Hallelujah!

Immediately, however, the doctor saw he had a problem. The baby had had a bowel movement in the amniotic fluid. This can be dangerous, especially when it has been in the water for a long period of time, because the baby drinks the contaminated water while still inside the mother.

The doctor and nurses began to work to suck out all the bad fluid he had swallowed, and praise God, they got it all! Except for the fact that he had a pointed head for about twenty-four hours and that he came out all covered with green slime, he was absolutely perfect!

The first miracle in bringing Lil' Harry into this world was overcoming the bad report that I was not even supposed to have children. When he got here, we had to overcome Satan's attempt to kill him by poisoning him and lodging him in the birth canal. But no matter what the enemy tried to do to Lil' Harry, Satan could not win!

Little Harry was strong from the very beginning of conception. He was not going to be defeated, and nothing was going to stop him from completing what God had created him to do and be! Harry Assad Salem means "Tiger of Peace," and from the very beginning of his existence this baby was living up to his name! Before we left the hospital we met with one more trial.

A woman had come into the hospital to try to steal our precious miracle from us. God is so wonderful, because He completely protected Lil' Harry from harm. This woman had called the hospital, explained she was our baby's grandmother, and wanted to know where he was. Thankfully, one of the security guards realized that Harry's mother was already in my room and my mother was still in Mississippi.

The security guard called Harry, who was in my room, to alert him. Then, when the woman came to the hospital, he tried to detain her by asking her some questions to give Harry time to get there and confront her. The woman became so agitated, she fled the hospital. (This was probably because she saw that gigantic angel with the big sword who was guarding Lil' Harry!)

Lil' Harry looked just like his daddy from the minute he was born, but we all recognized a dogged determination in his personality that was just like me. Harry and I had prayed from day one that he would have the best of both of us, physically, mentally, emotionally, and spiritually. Now that he is a big boy, we can honestly say he has all of our best traits!

Sometimes we as parents don't recognize these best traits in ourselves until we see them mirrored back in our children. Little Harry is very sensitive like his father, and very spiritually in tune like his mother. He is strong in his determination, and as far as he is concerned, he is rarely wrong! He has a great self image and loves God with all his heart. He received Jesus in his heart when he was five years old, and was so moved (and still is) by what Jesus did for him on the cross.

When he was six years old he asked us if he could receive "that Spanish prayer we pray every night." We explained that the language he wanted was given by receiving the Holy Spirit into his life. So he said, "OK, I want Him." We prayed together, he believed, and he immediately began speaking in his heavenly prayer language. He uses his prayer language almost daily without prompting by us. Both Harry and I recognize in our son a great longing to be close to the Father God, and we are so thankful.

Along with all of this spirituality came a very active, energized little boy with a very inquisitive mind and the ability to get into more trouble than I could ever imagine! From the very beginning Little Harry grew at a very rapid rate. He began taking steps without assistance as early as seven months and walked comfortably by nine months! This meant a lot of falling, bumping, and bleeding!

I wanted him to be perfect in every way, and because he was very much like me in his personality, I was very hard on him. Now I realize this was because he was my first child and I still had a lot to learn.

I learned that Lil' Harry did not "belong" to me, that he was just on loan from the Father. But the greatest thing I learned was this child had a will, a personality, and a character from the very first breath he breathed. I wanted to be able to mold him into a perfect human without his ever having to make a mistake. How silly of me. Now I know he has to go through everything in his life just like you and I do, bumps and all, if he is to develop into the man God has called him to be.

When Lil' Harry was two years old we went to a basketball game at Oral Roberts University. After the game he was running around, just being a typical little boy, when he fell and split his chin open. We had to take him to the hospital where the doctors tried to put stitches in his chin. But he was too scared, and so they butterflied the cut, put splints on both his arms to prevent him from pulling out the butterflies, and sent us all home.

What a nightmare! A two year old whose arms are immobile is not my idea of a fun time. This was devastating to both Harry and me. I had always hoped that my children would never have to go through some of the things I had been through like stitches and scars — especially on his face!

We were opening our first retail dress shop when Lil' Harry was four years old. He was with us as we were getting everything ready and, as usual, was climbing on something. In a matter of seconds he had climbed up on a metal cabinet and had pulled it over on himself! It came right across his chest and face and fell with full force on him. He could have been crushed under the weight of it! Thank God for the protection of the angels and for that barrel chest he inherited from his Granddaddy Harry!

Blood seemed to be everywhere. I have always prided myself in my ability to be calm in the midst of crisis. Well, was I wrong when it came to my first-born child and *his* blood. On the other hand, Harry was totally calm and collected. He told me to go and call the doctor.

I always have every phone number in the whole world in my head and at that moment I couldn't think of any number! Nothing would come to me. I was literally running from one store to the next in the shopping complex trying to think of our doctor's number. I was a complete wreck and pretty much a nut!

Finally, I thought of the number and called the doctor. Harry had Lil' Harry calmed down, and we started to the clinic. It was very obvious to both of us this was a serious cut. He was going to need many stitches right across his cheek and under his nose. This was not what I wanted for my children. NO SCARS, LORD! PLEASE, LORD, NO SCARS!

Daddy Harry continued to be calm and collected even though Lil' Harry continued to say, "Daddy, please fix the blood. Make it go away!" I know this had to be one of the hardest things Harry will ever go through as a father. There was a problem with one of his children and he was unable to fix it! Every word was breaking his heart.

Once we got to the doctor's office I was much better in control of the situation. I can handle the hospital part: stitches, needles, and the like. That's good because Harry can't handle any of that stuff! By the time they got Lil' Harry sedated and ready to sew him up, Daddy was green around the gills and ready to faint. That's when I took over. I helped them hold Lil' Harry down, clean and sew him up, and get him ready to take home. Isn't God funny the way He puts two people together? Harry handles the immediate crisis well and I handle the long-range clean up of the crisis. What a team!

Quickly I had to learn our son would survive scars on the outside and scars on the inside just as I had, and just as Harry had survived heartbreak after heartbreak in his life. Lil' Harry would have to go through whatever is in the plan for his life. I do want him to be what God has called him to be. The mother in me would love it if he could find God's will and stay under a protective glass jar at the same time!

After we were back home and had calmed down somewhat, I began to deal with my feelings. In all my life, in all the things I have had to go through to become what I am today, I never asked, "Why me, Lord?," "Where were You when I needed You?" or "I don't deserve this, Lord." Never once did these questions, comments, or feelings, come out of my mouth or even cross my mind.

But I have to tell you, when my child was hurt and scarred for the rest of his life, I said to the angels, "Where were you guys? Were you on a coffee break or something?" I was really angry with them. I have physically seen angels over the years. Not only do I know they exist, I know they work for us on this earth! It made me so angry when I thought those angels just stood around and let that metal cabinet fall on my precious baby's face! How they would allow that to happen was more than I could fathom!

I would love to tell you the Father God spoke up immediately in my heart and gave me the answer to all my questions, but it would not be factual. Actually, even if He had spoken to me I really doubt if I could or would have heard Him. At that time I was just too angry to hear! That was all there was to it. (Have you ever felt that way?)

Several days later, after I had calmed down and realized I do not own our children, nor can I interfere with God's plan for their lives, Harry pointed out to me that the angels had saved Lil' Harry's life. He might have been killed had it not been for those angels, because the doctor said the cabinet should have crushed his chest, broken his cheek, or put out his eye.

As I got my mind back on track, I began to realize the angels had been on duty after all. They weren't on a coffee break. They had saved Lil' Harry's life! I began to feel a peace and a calm come over me. I felt an assurance that the Father had everything under control. My job was to relax and quit trying to run the show.

I am not saying God caused that metal cabinet to fall on our son. My Bible says it is Satan who comes to steal, kill, and destroy. (John 10:10.) I am saying we don't know God's plan for the life of someone else, even our own children, or how the devil will attack them. We can't predict what it is going to take to mold them into the men and women of God they are to become. And remember, God always has a way of deliverance for us when things go wrong. (Romans 8:28.)

The scar is still on Lil' Harry's face, but he is so handsome you don't even notice it. And just like the scars on my face, they give him character and make him a little different from the rest of the human race — in a good way! His scar will remind him of how God protected him, just as my scars remind me of my miracle. He is so courageous, one little scar could never stop him from doing what God has called him to do, anyway!

We need to remember that many times what may look like defeat to the natural eye is really a war being won in the spirit realm. The one left standing at the end of the war is the winner. If we survive, if we are standing when the dust settles from the battle, we are the winners. Satan is defeated. Hallelujah!

You may be beaten up pretty badly, you may be bleeding, you may have a few scars. But if you are standing, you are the winner! Ephesians 6:13-14 (AMP) says:

> **Therefore put on God's complete armor, that you may be able to resist and stand your ground on the evil day [of danger], and, having done all [the crisis demands], to stand [firmly in your place]. Stand therefore [hold your ground], having tightened the belt of truth around your loins, and having put on the breastplate of integrity and of moral rectitude and right standing with God.**

Day after day I have become stronger and stronger because of Lil' Harry's personality. But he is a challenge in every way because of his strong character. He questions everything and takes nothing at face value. And the answer "because I said so" means absolutely nothing to him! I have had to remind him on a daily basis that I am the mother and he is the son.

From the time he was born he was constantly happy. I was so thankful he was in my life. I realize how often he completely accepts me just as I am. I don't have to perform for him. He loves me anyway. No matter how much or how little I do, his love for me is totally unaffected.

This is how I first began to get a tiny glimpse of the true love of the Father God for us, His children. When I became a parent I began to realize what it must have been like to give up your only son to suffer, be ridiculed, be tortured, and eventually die a violent death at the hands of people who only have bad things to say about you. Jesus willingly gave His life for these people. But the Father God willingly let Him do it.

God the Father actually wanted His only son to do this for people who were hateful, angry, mean, unfair, bitter, and horrible to His son. He knew they would be that way before He ever let Jesus come to the earth! This is so hard for me as a parent to imagine! We deserve so little of His love and yet He gives it so freely and without limitations.

As a mother I have a hard time telling Lil' Harry to be kind to boys at school who aren't nice to him. My first response is to tell him to belt them! (Great example, huh? I don't tell him this, but I think it!) We don't want anyone to ever hurt our children. And it makes no difference to a parent whether it is accidentally or intentionally.

I kept a journal about Lil' Harry when he was a baby. I repeatedly noted that I hoped I was making the right decisions concerning his discipline. You see, I was pretty hard on him from the time he was about two years old until he was around five years old.

Up until about age two he was the happiest, most fun loving, sensitive child I had ever known. None of these characteristics changed. They were just enhanced and strengthened as Lil' Harry's tremendous personality began taking root and as he came into his own nature.

When a child has a strong personality the parent sometimes thinks it is a *difficult* personality. We tend to be tougher on this type of character which is not always the best way to handle the child. I was definitely harder on Lil' Harry because of his strength. I had to learn that strength is a great asset in his life, and it's up to me to cultivate it, not destroy it.

The real problem for me was not in his looks. (He is the image of his father.) It was that in every other way — his nature, his personality, his persistence (stubbornness), his tenacity — he was just like me! Absolutely me! It was like looking into a mirror and seeing yourself just the way you really are before you learn to hide behind the manipulative traits life teaches you. When I realized there was someone on this earth exactly like me, I thought it was a terrible thing.

I could barely stand living with myself, trying to figure myself out and trying to survive my own driving nature. But to realize there is a carbon copy of me is a lot to handle. And this one is a male to boot!

I wanted him to be perfect. I wanted him to be everything I ever wanted to be, but with no mistakes, no trials, no tribulations, no problems. And I wanted his life to be trouble free, absolutely the opposite of mine. Sounds good, doesn't it? But do you know how unrealistic that is? And impossible!

Lil' Harry had to have the freedom to grow up, make his own choices, and become who God called and created him to be. This was not my second chance in life to correct everything I did wrong the first time around. No! No! That would be completely unfair to the child. It would never work. No one could ever love a child or be more thankful for a child than I have been for Lil' Harry, partly because I have learned so much.

Since I have had other children I realize another great truth. There are no set rules, no absolutes in child rearing. All children, and I mean ALL CHILDREN are completely different. You can't rear them the same, discipline them the same, feed them the same, or potty train them the same. NOTHING IS THE SAME! Just when you think you have it all figured out here comes the next one, and everything is different.

The Bible is the best instruction manual for training children. The principles of discipline and teaching children apply to every child in any situation. However, God's Word is generic, applying to all models, and we need the Holy Spirit to help us with the individual features of each unique child.

I have often wished I had a personalized manual, complete with all the little quirks and idiosyncrasies of that particular child, that came with every one of my children! The Holy Spirit helps me to take the principles of God's Word and temper them to each child.

This is definitely what I needed to do when Roman was born. . . .

3
Roman: Joy

When Harry and I got married and when Lil' Harry was born we were so excited. Our little family was just wonderful, and we had so much fun being together. We had a lot to learn about being parents, but we dove in head first and learned the best we knew how. The day came when we decided that Lil' Harry needed a sibling. He loved all of his cousins, but he needed someone he could grow up with. Harry and I both felt there was a real need that only another child could fill.

We began to plan what time of the year would be good to have a baby. I gave a lot of thought to what months I felt would be the most convenient to be pregnant. I considered the weather, my travel schedule, and other things. But it wasn't very long before we could tell Lil' Harry that we had a baby on the way. Daddy Harry was absolutely sure from the very beginning this baby was a boy. He wouldn't hear of anything else.

The pregnancy went beautifully and with no problems, just like when I was pregnant with Lil' Harry. I traveled and ministered until the eighth month with very little discomfort. I had only gained twenty pounds during my first pregnancy. By exercising regularly, I only gained twenty pounds the second time also. And I never had morning sickness with either one!

In November, on my way back from a church where I had been ministering, I began to experience my first problems. On the plane I began to have some false labor. At least, that's what I thought it was. I assumed it was from standing on my feet and ministering for several days. I figured if I sat back and relaxed and rested, it would stop.

The young lady traveling with me had been with me for several years and knew me very well. She began to question me and finally got me to tell her I was having contractions — and they were coming regularly. She rubbed my back for the longest time hoping it would make me feel better.

I finally told the stewardess I might be in labor. She assured me if they had to deliver the baby they were trained to do so, and for me not to worry. I was not worrying. I was praying!

First of all, I did not want to have the baby on an airplane. Secondly, I knew it was too early to have this baby. My friend and I prayed and agreed that my body would not respond to this labor, that I would not drop my fruit before its time (Malachi 3:11).

By the time we got to Dallas I was getting exhausted, but I knew we had Satan on the run. The pains were still coming, but my faith knew they would be of no effect. By the time we arrived in Tulsa my emotions were running rampant. When I saw Harry in the airport I started to cry because I was so tired. I could tell he was really concerned, but the labor had stopped by then and he took me home.

I went to the doctor the next morning and he checked me. He told me I needed to cancel all ministry dates until the baby came in January. I hated to do this, but it was the only way to be safe. The baby was my primary concern.

The months of November and December seemed to be so long. By Christmas Day I was sure the baby was ready to come! (I was sure, but the baby wasn't.) December passed and January came on the scene and still no baby. Don't get me wrong. I wasn't late. The baby wasn't due until the end of January or the first of February, but I just wanted this to be over! This attitude doesn't help your frame of mind, nor does it make the baby come any sooner!

By then I was in a sensitive mood all the time. I was irritable and short tempered, and was not easy to live with in any way. I was not used to being "on hold" where time is concerned. By not being able to work, the anxiety just compounded!

About one week before I was to deliver the baby, Oral Roberts released a book entitled, *A Prayer Cover Over Your Life,* and I began to read a chapter to Lil' Harry every night. I had already anointed our entire house with oil, but after reading Oral's book on the prayer cover, I felt led to do it again. I took some cooking oil out of the kitchen and began to re-anoint everything in our home.

Each time I anointed a door or a window in the name of the Father, the Son, and the Holy Ghost, I would go ahead and pray a prayer cover over each entry to our home. As I covered the house, I prayed a prayer cover over all of our properties and each family member. I felt that God was telling Harry and me that we needed extra protection, more than ever before. We were not afraid, but merely on our spiritual guard to protect our family from any onslaught of the enemy.

By the third week of January I was having regular contractions off and on all the time. I knew at any moment the "real thing" could begin. On Sunday, January 21st, I got out of bed in a terrible mood. Everything everybody said was the wrong thing to say. I called my friend, Denise. Although I don't remember the conversation, I'm sure I must have been in labor because I got mad at her. I have never been angry with her over anything before or since that day. But she just rubbed me the wrong way that morning — and I must have told her off!

She called Harry after we were finished talking and told him I must be in labor. He said she was probably right because I had already been crying, complaining, and in general airing every feeling I had. I was pretty hysterical and not a pretty sight!

That afternoon, Harry took me and Lil' Harry to the grocery store. I was miserable, but because I was not having anything of any importance in the contraction department, I thought shopping would be no problem. We bought groceries, brought them home, and unloaded them. Then I cooked supper and called some friends to come over for supper.

About the time we sat down to eat I got still long enough to realize that the contractions I had been having all day were regular enough to time. When I timed them they were three minutes apart! Can you believe that? After another forty minutes or so, Harry convinced me to call the doctor. I called and asked his answering service to find him, then went upstairs to clean up.

About this time Richard, Lindsay, and their children dropped by. (They always seem to show up when I need them most!) My doctor, "Dr. Mike," returned my call at 7:00 p.m. and I filled him in on the details. The contractions were harder by this time but I told Dr. Mike I wasn't ready to go to the hospital. After being in labor for such a long time with Lil' Harry, I was determined not to go to the hospital too early. Dr. Mike disagreed and told Harry and me to meet him at the hospital. I reluctantly agreed to go and finished packing my suitcase.

Our friends stayed with Lil' Harry, and Richard and Lindsay said they would join us at the hospital as soon as they made sure everything was settled with Lil' Harry. I called my friend and coach, Denise, and told her we were going to the hospital. (But I let her know I didn't think we would be staying!)

When Harry and I arrived at the hospital at 7:30 p.m., I refused to let him take my suitcase in because I was convinced this was not the real thing. By 7:45 Dr. Mike joined us and examined me. He convinced me this was *really* the "real thing" and that I was staying.

Denise and Lindsay came in shortly after and we got under way. I walked about a hundred miles that night in a circle around the nursery. (I might be exaggerating a little!) The labor was pretty powerful but not powerful enough to open my cervix the way it should. Around 10 p.m. Dr. Mike broke my water and wouldn't let me walk anymore.

Around 1 a.m. on the 22nd I was still having contractions but they weren't effective enough to open the cervix. Dr. Mike started me on Pitocin drip to intensify my contractions. And that's exactly what it did! The labor was hard and fast. There was definitely pain and lots of it.

I didn't complain. I began to concentrate on what I had to do to get the baby here as fast as possible. It crossed my mind to go home and forget the whole thing, but I figured out that was not really an option! So I decided to buckle down and get this thing over with as soon as possible.

About 2:30 a.m. I was ready to push, and by 3:14 a.m., January 22nd, 1990, Roman Lee Salem came into this world.

Because of the problems with Lil' Harry's birth, a neonatal specialist had been brought in toward the end of the delivery. Once Roman was born, the specialist and a few nurses took him from Dr. Ritze and laid him on a table to work on him, because he had swallowed some meconium while coming through the birth canal just as his brother had.

Within five minutes the specialist, nurses, and Harry took Roman out of the delivery room to an adjoining room where the specialist stuck a long tube down his nose and into his lungs. The doctor literally sucked on one end of the tube to try and suck the poisonous fluid out of the baby's lungs. The fluid was also behind his vocal chords and had stopped up one of his bronchial tubes.

About thirty minutes later (and much prayer and trusting God!) I got to see Roman and hold him. He was so sweet! From the very first moment I laid eyes on him, I knew he would always bring me great joy and happiness. His peaceful spirit moved me to great depths of feelings and I knew I would always love him deeply. He weighed eight pounds, eight ounces, and was 21 3/4 inches long. The circumference of his head was 13 1/2 inches, and his chest was 14 inches around. He had blue eyes, a lot of brown hair, and a very dark complexion.

Every four hours the nurses and doctors came into our room to try and loosen the stuff in his lungs that they couldn't get out when he was born. They would beat on his back with a little rubber mallet. It didn't lead to a restful stay in the hospital! To make matters worse, we weren't in the City of Faith with this birth, because it had closed only months before. We were so privileged to have the City of Faith when Lil' Harry was born.

Being in an unfamiliar hospital was a little unnerving from a security standpoint, so Harry had hired round-the-clock security guards to be at the room with Roman and me. Harry seemed to be more protective than ever, but I assumed it was because of the attempted abduction of Lil' Harry when he was born. What I didn't know until several years later was that I was being stalked by a man with the apparent intent to abduct me.

The day after I had given birth to Roman, Harry received a phone call from a detective from one of the nearby counties concerning a man they had recently arrested. This man had been caught after abducting two women with the apparent intent to kill them. After Harry and a friend of his, a former DEA agent, confirmed the validity of this story, they met with the detective at the Tulsa Police station.

Harry told the detective that I was unavailable to meet with them personally because I had just had a baby. The detective then proceeded to tell him that the man they had in custody had formerly been in prison. While in prison, this man had apparently constructed a journal with the names, photos, and addresses of women from newspaper and magazine articles.

Alongside the names of each of these women was a number, which the detectives realized was his "pecking" order. A Tulsa councilwoman, who bore a striking resemblence to me, was on the list. All these women were brunette, between 5'5" and 5'9", and had appeared on television or in local newspaper or pageant magazines over the previous year. Harry pointed out to the detective that the addresses of all the women on his list were near my office, and that if you lined all of them up side by side we looked like sisters!

From the information Harry obtained, this man had been stalking me and had all kinds of information about us. Ironically, when he was arrested for abducting the two women, he was in the vicinity of the hospital where I was having Roman. That was too close for comfort!

You might think that Harry should have talked to me about it or been a little more concerned, but this is something we had dealt with before and he felt it was not right to let the devil steal the joy of Roman's birth by bringing this to my attention. He knew that I had done everything spiritually by anointing the house and praying a prayer cover to protect us and he was doing everything possible in the natural to protect us.

Although Harry had told me nothing, the Holy Spirit knew what was going on! Now I know why I read Oral Roberts' book on the prayer cover to Lil' Harry each night just a week prior to Roman's birth and why I felt so compelled to pray at such great lengths over our home, properties, and household!

We had to stay an extra day in the hospital until we knew Roman's lungs were fine. Then Harry took us home to our good friend, Tracey (who had come to stay with us to help me and the baby), and to a most excited brother, Lil' Harry.

The next few months proved to be quite uneventful, thank God. I was so glad things were running smoothly and everything was beginning to fall back into place. With Tracey there to help, I was able to go back on the road traveling and ministering when Roman was six weeks old. It's never easy to leave a child to go back to work, but if you have capable people you can trust, it sure does help!

Harry is such a good father. He jumped right in making the transition between having one child to having two. Lil' Harry was also absolutely wonderful about the whole thing. He was so thankful to have a brother. His only problem was that he couldn't seem to understand Roman didn't come on this earth ready to run and jump and play! This took some explaining and careful watching. We wanted to make sure he didn't try to teach Roman to walk the first week!

We knew immediately that Roman was very strong, both in his body and in his personality. He was so sweet and precious, with a nature just like his father. When he began to walk it was obvious he was going to be the opposite of Lil' Harry. Lil' Harry was like me, bold, friendly, stubborn, aggressive. Roman, on the other hand, was tentative, reserved, gentle, careful, and cautious. He held on to things and took as few tumbles as possible. This was definitely not my nature. He reminded me of his father in so many ways, and I loved him totally. Now I realize how much harder I was on Lil' Harry because he reminded me of myself. Isn't hindsight wonderful?

It seemed that every entry I made into Roman's book was about how happy he made me, how much joy he brought into my life, and how content he made me. He was the total balance to Lil' Harry's personality. It dawned on me one day, while I was comparing the two personalities of our sons, that this must be why the Father God made each of us so different.

No two individuals are exactly the same. We are unique to the Father, and each of us brings Him great joy, great strength, great happiness. That was just what our boys were bringing to me. Each one has his own way of doing things, his own personality, and his own strengths and weaknesses. These differences were so much fun, as well as being challenging, frustrating and wonderful. Having two children so uniquely different showed me another aspect to the Father's personality and character, one more insight into the beauty of our heavenly Father! He loves individuals, not clones. He likes our little unique quirks which make us who we really are.

As a mother I quickly learned I was not perfect. And now I was a mother of two! I had to learn to prioritize every minute to insure that I spent suitable time with my children.

You see, I loved to work. My first loves had always been traveling, ministering and singing. But now the Father God began to show me that although my ministry was doing great and that it was effective, it was not His desire that my husband and our children should suffer for the gospel's sake. God would never destroy a family to promote a ministry.

I realized that the greatest thing I could ever do was written in Proverbs 22:6. I should train up my children in the way they should go and when they are old they will not depart from it. As I taught my children to love God, hear His voice and follow His lead, I would be accomplishing more in the long run than I could ever do on my own. Reproducing the call of God through our children has got to be the most satisfying revelation God has ever given me.

Harry and I pray this over our children every night:

"We anoint you in the Name of the Father, the Son, and the Holy Spirit. We plead the blood of Jesus over you, under you, and all around you. We put a wall of prayer around you and a prayer covering over you. We ask you, Father, to put four angels over our children to guard, guide, direct, and protect them."

"We thank you, Lord, that all our children shall be taught of the Lord and great shall be their peace and undisturbed composure (Isaiah 54:13)." Our children dwell in the secret place of the Most High and abide under the shadow of the Almighty. They will say of the Lord, You are my refuge and my fortress: my God in Him will we trust."

We have learned to continue to read scriptures over our children until we feel peace in our hearts that we have covered whatever situations they are facing. We also began to teach our children how to pray the Word of God over themselves and each other. Teaching them to pray the Word of God at an early age is vital to their spiritual maturity and survival in these last days.

Harry and I also spend time explaining Bible stories to our children. Lil' Harry has always been especially interested (probably because he is older) and his tender heart began to emerge early. One day right before Easter he came home from kindergarten and told us to sit down on the couch. He wanted to do a play for us. We sat down and he began. We had no idea what to expect. He has always had the biggest imagination!

He began portraying Jesus on the donkey during Passover, then in the garden begging for this cup to pass from Him, then on the cross, then the resurrection, then the ascension! We were amazed at the memory of this child. I cried and asked him to do it again. He repeated this fifteen minute performance all over again word for word. We couldn't imagine who had taught him all of the dialogue, and how he could remember all the lines and the motions. He repeated it over and over for everyone who came by our home that night.

The next day when I picked him up from school I asked his teacher which of them had been teaching him this play for Easter. She said she had no idea what I was talking about! When we finally got to the bottom of it, we learned he had been watching a puppet video called "Here Comes Jesus" by Peter Enns Ministry. Lil' Harry had memorized that video, word for word, complete with action and motions! I can't take the credit for "teaching" this material to Lil' Harry, but I'm glad we make sure our children watch Christian videos.

When you put the Word of God into your children it will take root, because the Word is alive and full of power. You don't have to make it happen. You just have to be obedient and do what God has taught us to do. Train up a child. Train up a child. TRAIN UP A CHILD!! The spirit of the child will grab hold of the Word of God and run with it.

We have learned that training is not something we do once or twice and expect it to take root. We have to do it over and over again. When someone is training an animal to do tricks they will work with that animal for hours on end, day after day, sometimes week after week just to learn one trick. Therefore, we could not expect our children to be able to grasp what we wanted them to learn without effort on our part.

The lesson that we're learning is that training is as much hard work for the trainer as it is for the one being trained! It takes patience and endurance. This is the only way for training to be effective. When it comes to our children we have had to learn to give them our time. That means quality time, of course, but we also have to make sure that the *quantity* is sufficient. Repetition is a great teacher! We've found it's easy to get discouraged, but we refuse to give up. Harry and I stick with it, because their little lives are worth it!

Lil' Harry says to me every time I am getting ready to leave on a ministry trip, "When are you going to let me go and preach?" I tell him when he is ready he can go. I'm sure it won't be too much longer. His heart is so open to the Father God. He is so sensitive to the voice of the Father. We're seeing that when we train our children, God will do the rest!

For every challenge Lil' Harry has put in my life, Roman has only brought me joy. But that old saying, "the squeaky wheel gets the grease," has a lot of truth in it. We need to be very careful that the child that causes you the most work doesn't get most of your attention. If we are not cautious about this, that is the way it will be.

Don't get me wrong. Lil' Harry is not a problem child. Not at all! He just presents challenges to me as a parent because of his personality, drive, and aggressiveness. The very things that will make him a strong man of God are the traits that need bending (not breaking) toward God!

Roman, on the other hand, seemed to be the ideal child. At least it seemed that way until he was about three. At age three several personality traits began to emerge that weren't completely positive: he has a very strong will; when he believes he is right, he will not say he is sorry; and he will not repent until he *really* believes he should.

Once again, these are very strong, wonderful characteristics for the future. But they can sometimes present a challenge to a parent in bending these traits toward God. This is difficult, but never impossible. It just takes work and consistency. Children are like God's Word — it is simple, but not easy! Faith is simple, but not easy! Children are simple, but not easy!

When Roman was only two years old or so, he woke up in the night very sick to his stomach. Instead of whining and crying, I heard him screaming something at me. I came running down the hall, trying to figure out what he was saying. By the time I got to his room I had finally interpreted the words of this heartfelt cry.

He was sitting up in bed, violently sick. Instead of feeling sorry for himself (like so many adults would have at this time), he was screaming "Mama, pray! Mama, pray!" He came out of his sleep knowing what to do in a crisis. How many people do you know who wake up out of a deep sleep knowing to pray when something is wrong? *Especially* impressive at age two!

Several more times during the night we would get him settled down and he would fall back to sleep. Then he would wake up screaming the same thing, "Mama, pray! Mama pray!" Even though his healing did not come immediately, he never changed his request. He never got tired of asking me to pray. He never said "Why isn't God healing me?" He stayed consistent with his faith, his prayer, and his confession.

Harry and I were seeing how, in teaching a child to believe God's promises, one of the most vital parts is to teach the child never to quit believing. NEVER! Teach him, instead, to continue to believe until he has what he needs from the Father — no matter how long it takes.

We also saw how our children were learning from our example more than from our words. Teaching them is important, but example is much more effective for lasting results. You see, our children knew what God had done for me. They knew that my legs were uneven for a long time after the car accident when I was eleven years old. They knew I never gave up believing that God was going to heal me, and six years later my legs were made the same length by the miracle power of God. They look at me now, completely healed and restored, and can understand the importance of holding on to their faith — no matter how long it takes — to receive what they are desiring.

Our children are our heritage from the Father (Psalm 127:3). We want to make sure our children know how to walk in God's promises, how to trust that their Father God will always be there for them. We realize we can't just sit down and read the *King James Version* of the Bible to our children and expect them to listen and be interested. But we can talk the promises of God in our everyday conversation. We can pray the promises of God out loud when we pray over our children. They are listening, and Roman's tenacity that night surprised us about what our children were absorbing!

When our children bring their problems to us to be solved (in our house this happens all day long), Harry and I have learned to answer with the Word of God. We can't say, "thus saith the Lord," of course. But we do say, "The Bible says this about your problem," and proceed to give them some food for thought as to what to do.

Through instructing our children, Harry and I have also come to understand that we can't answer our children with the Word of God if we are not studying the Word on a regular basis ourselves! A knowledge of the Bible is vital if we are going to teach our children to live godly, joyful lives. This, in itself, is enough to motivate us to study, pray, and meditate on God's Word!

I think you can see how, as he has challenged and encouraged us to grow in our faith and trust in the Father God, Roman has filled our lives with joy!

4
Malachi Charles: Compassion

It is amazing how busy you can get trying to be a perfect mother, wife, minister, businesswoman, and so forth. It is so easy to forget what is really important in life and get your priorities all out of order. *Setting* priorities is often easy, but *keeping* them in line is difficult. Satan takes every opportunity to distract us from our true purpose and calling. That is why it is so vital to stay close to the Father God on a personal basis, not just as a minister, but (more importantly) as a little child.

More than anything else God wants and deserves our praise, our fellowship, and our time. The most valuable part of you that you can give anyone is your time. At least, in my life that is true.

Before I had Roman I received a prophecy that the anointing in my life would increase with the birth of each child. It did! After Lil' Harry was born you could see and feel a definite difference in the ministry. It was obvious God's hand was upon me, and I was doing what I was called to do. He was blessing me in every way.

When I got pregnant with Roman the increase in anointing was immediately evident. After his birth there was another surge of growth in my walk with the Lord. Just waiting on God has become a way of life for me. I learned years ago that the call of God and His direction in my life is so wonderful to have. But His perfect timing is more important. I have never tried to hurry up what God is doing in me and through me. It's been enough for me to be used at whatever level He sees fit.

Harry and I began to get the urge to have another baby when Roman turned two years old. I must admit that Harry was much more ready than I. I had just begun to get a goodnight's sleep and I wasn't ready to give that up. But I have come to realize there are only a few things I can give Harry that no one else can give him. One thing I can do for him that no one else can is having his baby and rearing that child in the admonition of the Lord. So when he began to give me the indication that he was wanting to "fill his quiver" with another child (Psalm 127:4,5), I began to look at my travel schedule to figure out when would be the best time to have this baby. We decided a May pregnancy would put the baby here at a good time.

I was on the road ministering when I knew I had ovulated. I prayed God would keep everything in place until I could get home. I started my period two weeks later when I expected to be pregnant, and I was not happy about it. But getting frustrated has never changed anything or helped any situation, so I put those feelings out of my head and began to plan for the next month.

The time came for my next period and guess what? It didn't start. I went to the lab and had a pregnancy test after I was a few days late, and sure enough I was pregnant. I continued to work on a video I was putting together, and I continued to travel and preach. That weekend, I went to Hawaii to minister. When we were finished that Sunday, we flew home overnight.

As soon as we got home, I made an appointment to see the doctor. I was very tired, but I attributed it to being in the early stages of pregnancy. Being thirty-five years old didn't help, either! But after the doctor's appointment, I began to spot a little. This had never happened to me, but I didn't think much of it because I was spotting very little.

The next morning I was on Richard and Lindsay's daily television show, and I really began to bleed. I wasn't sure what I should do, so I asked Lindsay. She told me to get off my feet and call the doctor. I told her I had already called the doctor but he was out of town.

By the time I got home I was bleeding a lot more, so I called the doctor's office and requested to see anyone! One of Dr. Mike's colleagues examined me and told me he felt I had lost the baby. I was pretty upset but, for some reason, my faith was so high that I refused to believe this baby was gone. I couldn't accept it. I wouldn't accept it. I have a hard time losing at anything, especially a fight with the devil.

At home I lay in bed, praying and confessing and believing. I just wouldn't give up. No matter what anybody told me I kept believing.

On Thursday night I went to the bathroom about midnight and I dropped a clot that I knew was the baby. It wasn't doubt or unbelief, it was just a fact that my spirit knew to be true. I knew this was our baby. Our little sweetheart's spirit had just passed through my flesh and had ascended to heaven to be with Jesus.

We took the specimen to the lab where it was confirmed that this was the fetus. Harry and I both were devastated. I didn't know how to lose. I didn't know how to accept defeat. All I knew how to do was keep believing. But there was nothing left to believe for. I just didn't know what to do. Harry was hurting too, but I wasn't much help to him.

As we both began the grieving process we learned something very important. It is very difficult to grieve over someone without a name. The Bible says we will be known in heaven as we are known on the earth (1 Corinthians 13:12), and it dawned on me that I didn't want our baby to go throughout eternity without a name. I shared this with Harry. Naming our baby gave him a reality, an identity. It is very important in the grieving process to be able to focus the grief on something or someone so the grieving can have a beginning and an end.

We named the baby "Malachi Charles." Malachi, because Harry loved it, and Charles, after his grandfather on his mother's side. (There was one light moment when we wondered, "What if, when we all get to heaven, the baby turns out to be a girl!" Wouldn't that be funny? Oh, well, Harry was still so sure all his children would be boys!)

Not long after this baby had gone to heaven, I woke up in the middle of the night and knew something or someone was in the room with Harry and me. I sat up in bed and tried to focus my eyes in the dark.

As I sat on the edge of the bed I saw a dark, hooded and robed figure standing by the door of our bedroom. I realized this was not an angel because angels give off tremendous light. The Holy Spirit spoke in my heart and told me this was the spirit of death.

I promptly stood up, marched over to the bathroom and flipped on the light. I spoke to that dark form and told it, in no uncertain terms, to leave our home and never return. I told it I knew it had just come and taken our baby, but there was *no one* else for it to be concerned with. I commanded it in the Name of Jesus to go and never return. As it turned around and vanished through the wall, I knew in my heart it would not be back. The funny thing about all of this is Harry slept through the whole thing! Next time, Honey, WAKE UP!

The grieving was eventually over. I can't say it was an easy time, but it got easier every day as we accepted that we had a child already in heaven and realized this was one Satan would never tempt or hurt in any way! Hallelujah!

We realized that even in the loss of not having this child here on earth with us, we had not lost anything to the devil, nor would we ever really lose anything to him. Our precious Savior and Lord, Jesus, made it possible for even death to be put under our feet in victory. (See I Corinthians 15:54,55.)

The major impact this experience had on me, however, was very deep and far-reaching. For the first time in my life, I began to experience what the compassion of God for his hurting children really is, not only for myself, but toward others.

Compassion had never been one of my strong personality traits. I had always felt everyone needed to make the right choices in their lives, regardless of their circumstances, and go on living. In some ways this is a good way of looking at things, but many times people just need to be loved and held. They need to be given the opportunity to hurt and grieve without being told what to do!

After we lost Malachi, I began to see a real change in my attitude toward other hurting people. I began to see the compassion, love, and patience God had with me. I have always wanted to be like God, so I made a quality decision to focus more on people and less on what I thought they should be doing to overcome their problems.

This change of focus gave me a completely new perspective on hurting people. I realized that grieving is a vital part of healing. Without grief we hide the hurt under a scab of deep-seated pain. This hidden pain can turn into a multitude of problems, from anger and bitterness to actual sickness in your body!

I don't believe it is God's best for us that we cover up or hide our hurt and grief. He wants us to face all our emotions so that we may be completely restored in His love and compassion. And the more we seek after God and His ways, more of *Him* will begin to emerge and we will see less of *us*.

Perhaps we have gotten too hung up on the characteristics of the four basic personalities (choleric: "my way"; sanguine: "the fun way"; melancholy: "the right way"; and phlegmatic: "the easy way"). These four categories give us a place to run and say, "That's just the way I am. Everyone must accept me." This is not true!

Our "natural" personality should never be a crutch to keep us the way we are or to give us an excuse for our weaknesses. Our natural attributes should be a foundation on which to build a beautiful person. I want to be more like Jesus and less like me!

God tells us in His Word we are to die to self and imitate Jesus. (See 1 Thessalonians 1:7; 1 Timothy 4:12; Titus 2:7; Galatians 2:19; Romans 6:7-11.) As we do this, we have nowhere to hide. By regularly allowing the Holy Ghost to scrutinize and instruct us, we will begin to become more like the Jesus we love and serve.

Compassion may not be one of my strong "natural" traits, but it is a supernatural trait of Jesus. Because I am now in Him, I not only have the *ability* and *right* to be compassionate, but if I am obeying God's Word, I have the *obligation* to be compassionate to everyone I meet every day!

I have never lost a child after it was born, nor have I ever aborted a baby, but I now know how much pain people who have experienced these things go through, and I can tell them that there is healing, forgiveness, and complete deliverance from the "spirit of grief." God can and will restore us to health — physically, emotionally, spiritually, and mentally — if we will only trust Him to do so!

You do not have to be burdened down under guilt of "what you should have done." God will forgive you if you need forgiveness and immediately restore you to a right relationship with Him and to a right thinking mind (righteousness). You are so special and valuable to God!

We cannot live our lives allowing our futures to be distorted and tormented by our pasts. We need to learn to put our pasts behind us with the help of the Holy Spirit, and see our futures with *God's best plans* in our minds! This is the beautiful fruit of compassion. It's not just feeling someone else's pain, but helping them go through the pain and then move into peace and hope for the future.

I may never have known this rich aspect of the character of Christ in my life if I had not had the privilege of conceiving Malachi. Thank You, God, for bringing him into my life and using his sweet, short life here on earth to teach me compassion!

Our wedding day,
May 10, 1985

Lil Harry's birth
March, 1986

Roman's birthday, June, 1990

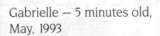

Gabrielle — 5 minutes old,
May, 1993

Christmas 1994
Roman, Harry III,
Gabrielle

5
Gabrielle: Healing

About two months after Malachi went to be with the Lord, we decided to try again. The second week of September I got pregnant. As usual, I conceived without any problem and felt fine. Because I had no morning sickness with any of my previous pregnancies, I never expected to have any with this one.

My travel schedule was very heavy, and once again I was trying to get an exercise video finished before I began to "show." During the last weekend of October I flew to Virginia Beach, Virginia, to minister in a wonderful women's conference. I ministered on Friday night, then flew to Los Angeles, California, early the next morning to be with the entire Richard Roberts Crusade Team. Richard and Lindsay were having a weekend crusade at Melody-land Church. I arrived in Los Angeles just in time to hurry straight to the church.

I spoke to a women's conference that Saturday afternoon. I was extremely tired, but it is my nature to always do what I am asked to do. I love ministering and have always taken advantage of every opportunity, no matter how stressful it may be to my body. After the meeting, we only had a short time to run back to the hotel, get cleaned up for the evening service, and get a bite to eat.

I had been fighting the flu for several days, so by this time my body was getting weak and I was losing my voice. The service started and I got up to sing. I wasn't much help to the team because I had almost complete laryngitis. By the

Sunday morning service there wasn't any reason for me to even try to help. I was feeling extremely tired and run down. After the services were over, Harry and I flew home, hoping to get some rest.

There wasn't any time for rest though. (That has always been my problem. I never have known when to stop and smell the roses!) We got home late Sunday night and Wednesday morning I repacked my suitcase and got back on a plane to fly to another women's conference.

Kim, a friend of mine, was traveling with me. It was her first trip with me and we were looking forward to being together. We talked all the way from Tulsa to Dallas. When we arrived in Dallas we checked the monitor to see the gate information for our connecting flight. All at once, from the waist down, I felt the hottest blood gush from my body and cover my pants. I was a mess.

I hadn't had any warning. Nothing! But that was the least of my problems. I reached for Kim and said, "Kim, it looks like I'm losing the baby." Still, I was pretty calm as Kim quickly guided me across the hall to the nearest bathroom. The entire time we were walking to the bathroom we prayed in the Spirit. We were already releasing our faith for a miracle. Somehow we both knew if God did not intervene, the baby was not going to make it.

I hadn't bled this much in an entire week when I lost Malachi Charles only a few months before. I was covered in blood. In the bathroom, I examined myself and discovered a clot about the size of a coffee cup. I held it in my hand. I just knew this was my baby.

Kim immediately went out to get help. She was back within a couple of minutes with a nurse who assured me the paramedics were on their way. The nurse tried to get me to give her the clot I was still holding in my hand, but I refused. The paramedics came within five minutes and they also tried to get the clot from me. I didn't give it up until one of the men convinced me they would take good care of it, and promised me they would take it to the hospital with us.

I really can't explain the way I felt at this time. I was kind of numb, I guess. I was on the stretcher in the back of the ambulance with one of the paramedics and Kim was in the front with the other one. I wasn't sure what was happening, and for some reason I just carried on a casual conversation.

Kim called Harry. Somehow she was able to locate him where he was having lunch. He immediately went to the airport and headed to Dallas. Harry hadn't been able to hear Kim very well. All he knew was that I was in an ambulance on my way to the hospital, that I was hemorrhaging, and that he was to get to Dallas quickly. He had no idea if I had been in an accident, if it was something to do with the baby, or what!

Within a few minutes we arrived at the emergency entrance of the hospital. They wheeled me into an examining room and a doctor came in. After we talked for a few minutes, he said he was pretty sure I had miscarried. He took a look at the blood clot I had brought with me and told me that in all probability this was the fetus. I was still bleeding profusely, so the doctor did a pelvic exam and confirmed that I had lost the baby.

After another hour or so, the bleeding was not letting up, so the doctor ordered an ultrasound to diagnose the source of the bleeding. As I waited for the test, a nurse came in and tried to console me. She told me this was all for the best, it really wasn't a baby yet and I shouldn't be too upset about it. She said this was just the way the body rids itself of a problem.

Well, this nurse will never say these things to a patient again! She was just what I needed to get my faith kicked back into gear and to get my focus back on the Lord and onto what I know to be true. I told her in no uncertain terms that she didn't know what she was talking about.

A child was in my womb from the second the seed was fertilized by the sperm. I told her my God is a big God who can overcome any mountain (Psalm 139:13-16, Mark 11:23-24)! By the time I got to the end of my speech I was preaching. The nurse immediately apologized. She said no one had ever pointed out these things to her with such conviction and she would not ever say these things to anyone again.

Kim went with me as I went to do the ultrasound. She had been praying in the Spirit the whole time. As I went in, Kim stayed out in the waiting room to pray. The doctor in charge of the ultrasound put me on the table, got his equipment ready and put the machine on my tummy. When the previous doctor had done the pelvic exam he had discovered a tumor on my cervix. The doctor doing the ultrasound confirmed that the tumor was there and saw several more on my right ovary. He was looking all around in my abdomen area when he said, "Well, the baby is fine."

"What!" I turned around to see what he was seeing on the monitor. I saw on the ultrasound screen this wonderful little baby, kicking and flailing around as big as can be right in my womb! Praise God! Nothing anyone had said to me in the last few hours meant anything to me. I had not miscarried the baby. The baby was not gone! I had passed a tumor. The baby was still alive and living in me!

I got so excited that I shouted, promptly alerting Kim out in the hall that something wonderful was going on in our little room. She ran in and started praising God with me. I think the doctor thought he had a couple of kooks on his hands, but we didn't care what anyone thought. My baby was alive and living in me. My baby would live and not die. My baby would declare the works of the Lord in his/her life (Psalm 118:17). From this moment on nothing could deter my faith. No one could take the dream of this child away from me.

I was taken back to the other side of the hospital where the original doctor was waiting for the report. I was very excited, to say the least, as I told him the baby was fine. But the doctor was not swayed by my enthusiasm, telling me it didn't matter what I had seen. I was bleeding too much to have any hope that the baby would live. He said there was NO HOPE for my baby to survive.

Can you imagine that? To tell me there was no hope at this point was a waste of words! I had already seen this child, and nothing was going to steal my dream of this baby now! Nothing was going to stop me from having this baby. My faith was refreshed, and I knew no matter what anyone said this baby was going to live!

By this time my precious husband had arrived in Dallas and found Kim and me at the hospital. When he came into the room, he looked so relieved to see me. I blurted out that the baby was fine, and we weren't going to lose this one. Harry told me Satan kept telling him that I was going to be dead and that he was going to have to rear our boys by himself.

You can never expect Satan to leave you alone, especially when you are in a crisis situation. This is when he is going to take every advantage to try to lie to you, to get fear started in your thought life, to take away your hope and faith by the infiltration of doubt and negative thoughts. Don't let him get away with it! He has no rights to you or to your future. Remind him regularly that you belong to God and he can't touch you. He hates to be reminded that you are covered in the blood of Jesus!

The doctor wasn't nearly as optimistic as I was, but I didn't care. He gave us the option of staying in the hospital or going to the hotel across the street. Of course, I chose the hotel, because then Kim and Harry could stay with me. I wanted all the positive faith I could get around me.

Too many people facing a desperate situation forget to build themselves up during the crisis. They start dwelling on the problem and forget to focus on the answer. The only thing that will help you at this point is to focus on the answer. The problem will get bigger and bigger if you don't get your eyes off of it. Don't tell God about your big problem; tell your problem about your BIG GOD!

Whatever you are looking at is what is growing in your life. This is why you have the greatest opportunity to practice your faith when you are in a situation of great testing and trial. How do you practice your faith? You use it when it's not convenient. You use it when it's not easy. You use it when all else seems to have packed up and gone home!

Immediately I had a great opportunity to kick the devil in the teeth by the words I was about to speak. When I saw the baby on the ultrasound, it sparked my faith into action. The doctor said there was no hope, but God says, **all things are possible to him that believeth** (Mark 9:23)! All I had to go on was what I knew to be true. I knew God's Word **would not return to me void** (Isaiah. 55:11), and I was about to prove that in my life and in the life of this baby!

Harry took Kim and me over to the hotel and checked us in. The doctor told me to lie completely flat, preferably without even a pillow under my head! This was so hard for me, but I was determined to be a good patient and do everything I was told to do. The doctor had said I might not be able to leave Dallas for a long time and wouldn't even commit to how long that time might be.

After twenty-four hours, the bleeding was beginning to slow down a little. Harry called a friend to bring our van from home because I couldn't fly. I laid down in the back the entire trip home. This was just the beginning of a very long journey the Lord was about to use to teach me how to listen and learn from Him in every situation.

I wanted to be well immediately. Within a few days I was frustrated and ready to get out of bed. I was trying to be good and have a good attitude, but with every minute I looked for an opportunity to prove I was completely well. I wanted to get up!

Harry was taking care of everything and doing a wonderful job with the children. Tracey was also there to take care of my every desire. But nothing made me happy. I have always been self sufficient. No one ever had to take care of me. I have always been able to take care of everyone else. I hated this reversal of roles and I was not dealing with it well. Harry finally admitted it was like trying to live with Godzilla in a cage!

After about two weeks, Thanksgiving was upon us. It has always been a tradition in our family for everyone to come to our house for Thanksgiving dinner, and Harry was not about to change the tradition just because I was out of commission. He said he had always done the Thanksgiving dinners before we were married, and he could do it now. So he did!

He and Tracey did all the cooking: turkey, mashed potatoes, gravy, casseroles, breads and desserts! I was stuck in the bed and was no help at all! Everyone came to our house and we had a feast. Harry had done it all without me!

I hated that he could take care of things without me. I felt he really didn't need me. But I finally concluded that maybe God could show me some things while He had me still long enough to hear — if I would lighten up! That is when I began to learn about faith all over again.

Of course, every time I would begin to feel a little better, I would jump up and start doing things again. Not too smart! Then I would start bleeding again and have to go back to bed. This cycle was getting old. One day right after Christmas I finally gave up. I actually felt myself relax as I said, "Okay, God, let's use this time constructively to accomplish something."

I began to plan all the things I could do while lying in bed. I could write this book on my children I had wanted to start. I could write a book on angels since I had been having visitations from angels for almost a year. I could finish the music project I so desperately needed to finish.

On and on I went with my great plans. I thought just sitting still before the Lord would be so unproductive. I couldn't imagine God ever being happy with that, at least not until later, when I understood the wisdom of Psalm 46:10. **Be still, and know that I am God.** I had always lived my life trying to be productive in order to please everyone around me — including God. I hadn't gotten hold of the truth that He loved me regardless of what I could do for Him.

As I started trying to accomplish my plans, nothing would happen. I couldn't get started on anything. My creative juices just wouldn't flow. I couldn't seem to get it together! This was not like me at all! I had always been able to accomplish more than anyone I knew, and all of a sudden I was just floating along accomplishing nothing! I was getting frustrated and beginning to get angry about the whole situation.

Finally, I went to God and He began to talk to me. (He would have talked to me earlier if I had gone before Him instead of trying to make things happen on my own!) He told me He wanted me to rest before Him. He was not impressed with my schedule, nor was He moved by my "busyness." He began to impress upon me that His love for me was not measured by how much I did for Him. He loved me if I never did another thing for Him. He loved me if I couldn't do anything!

You might be thinking any idiot should know this! But for some reason, even though I had lived and loved God all these years, even though I had taught everyone else that God's love is unconditional, it never dawned on me that I really didn't believe it for myself. I thought I had to do all that was humanly possible for God to continue to love me and use me for His kingdom. What a revelation as I finally got a real grasp on this truth. He loves me! He loves me! He loves me!

From then on, I spent time every day, a lot of time, alone with my Father God. I got to the point where all I wanted to do all day, every day, was read His Word, pray, be quiet before Him, and just rest in Him. Ohhhh, how good it felt to lie in His arms. I became aware of how much He loves me and likes to be with me, even more than I love Him and want to be with Him. This was the beginning of my real healing.

You see, as a child I had gone through many negative things. Many of us have a story to tell. Everyone has some things in his or her past to overcome, areas for God to heal. But I had already received so much healing that I honestly thought I was completely healed in every area. But this wasn't true.

When I was a little girl, I had been in a terrible car wreck. For six years one of my legs was shorter than the other. Many people know of that miraculous healing. But there was a story people did not know, a deep secret of a hurt I had received when I was a little girl, a hurt that I took only to God. I was in my late twenties when God began to heal the wounds of sexual abuse.

As a little girl I had been sexually abused by someone I loved very much, a person I considered to be "a good man." He was a very good man, but he had a very deep and bad problem. For years I kept this deep, dark secret to myself. I felt God surely couldn't love me, and this is why I had worked so hard to win God's approval. I thought if I accomplished enough "things" then He would be proud of me no matter what had happened when I was a child.

As a result I felt that little girls didn't have "normal" lives, and that they were never safe from anybody, even "good" people. I was really confused about whom I could trust. Consequently, I trusted no one. I had become accustomed to this wall in *my* life. But I was not ready to deal with the emotional pain that someone might hurt my little girl. That's why I always believed I would only have boys! I thought God would let me keep hiding from my fears. Was I ever wrong!

Somehow I thought I was completely well in this area. I had ministered to abused people for several years and had felt a real release of my own hurt and pain. But God was not finished with me yet!

When this baby was conceived I was sure it would be another boy, especially having two boys already. And Harry was so sure all of our children would be boys, he would never hear of anything but "boy confessions." That was fine with me.

We had an ultrasound done in the spring and it showed this baby was most probably going to be a girl. Harry was sure this was a mistake. I didn't want to deal with the possibility the baby might be a girl, so I agreed with him that the doctor was probably wrong. A few weeks later the doctor did another ultrasound. This one also showed that this baby was unmistakably a girl!

A girl. This hit me like a ton of bricks! In my mind, girls didn't have a lot of hope to be what I called NORMAL! Normal is an odd word, I guess, but to me it meant no pain, no abuse, no confusion, and no hurt. Being "normal" meant having a safe place to hide from anyone and anything that could destroy your life. I didn't want a child of mine to go through anything like I had gone through. Consequently I was afraid to have a girl!

I got before God and said, "God, are You sure?" Isn't it funny how we question God when we don't want to deal with something? Harry was really fine about having a girl. (He just wouldn't admit it at the time.) But for me the root was much deeper than just gender. The root was abuse. And I still held on to a lie of Satan, that girls couldn't be called of God.

As a little girl I had cried before God and felt His call upon my life, but I believed only boys could be called to preach. Still, I felt this uncontrollable desire to preach and minister God's Word to hurting people. I wanted to be a boy so I could preach — but there was more!

Now I realize part of this strong longing and desire to be a boy stemmed from my thinking that only little girls were abused, that little girls weren't safe from people. I wanted to be a boy so that nothing could harm me! In my mind, I equated being female with pain, and mental and emotional crippling.

You might be saying, "Wow, You sure did hide this well." Yes, I did! When you have been abused, you learn to live in secret. You learn to hide from the world letting people see only what you want them to see. I didn't want my daughter to have to go through pain. God very gently began to pull off one more layer of my scar and unhealed pain until I faced the fact that I had not dealt with the last layer of my hurt. He began to show me that what I had gone through had nothing to do with my being a girl.

Satan had lied to me and kept me in fear that I would have a female child. Now I had to face the fact that God's will had to be fulfilled through this child I was carrying. I had no right to predict the sex of this child, to confess the sex of this child or even to wish for a certain sex of this child. All I had the right to do was to carry this child in my womb, to rear this child in the ways of the Lord, to teach this child how to hear God's voice and to trust God enough to perform His perfect will in this child.

I had learned to trust God in my own life. Now was the time to learn to really trust Him with my children. ALL OF MY CHILDREN!

As I began to work through my feelings, I realized God was healing the last few layers of the scar that had been on my heart since I was a little girl. All the hidden feelings of hurt, anger, and distrust of others were beginning to fade away. God was using this little girl within my womb to show me the ultimate love the Father has for His children. He was using this precious angel to show me that His plan goes on regardless of Satan's attacks against us. Once again God was showing me, this time through my baby, that His abilities are not limited to man or to man's thinking.

How wonderful to know that, not only has He given me this wonderful, beautiful little girl, but He is also using this precious one to help me receive healing from abuse. What a great revelation to realize that my daughter can have a normal life, that she can do what God has called her to do, and that she does not have to be subject to problems that are handed down from one generation to the next. These problems are called generational curses. Harry and I are doing all we know to do to make sure that nothing will be passed down from us to any of our children except blessings, blessings, and more blessings! (Deuteronomy 28:2-14.)

Since I became a mother, I have learned more about stopping generational curses. Most of us want our children to have the very best they can possibly have, and I don't want my children carrying around any excess emotional baggage. As parents we must make sure our children are as protected as possible from things in our past. We have the right to rebuke Satan and command him to get his hands off God's property. After he is exposed and his power is broken, he has no legal right to hang onto our lives. And he can't harass the next generation, either, at least not as a generational problem.

Perhaps you are thinking Cheryl Salem has gone off the deep end. But let me show you what I mean. When you go to the doctor's office for a routine checkup, you immediately fill out a medical history. You have to declare every illness that has affected you or anyone else in your family up to three generations back. (After doing this, you're worried about everything — from migraines to cancer!) If Satan can get you thinking about what *might* happen to you, he has an open door to enter your body and your life.

Before I brought a little girl into the world, I wanted to be healed in every part of my life, but particularly in the area of being afraid of having a daughter. As God began to heal me — this doesn't always happen overnight — I began to realize I was slowly being released of the fears I had held for my daughter. As the weeks of the pregnancy came to a close and I knew the time was drawing near, I began to look forward to her arrival. All of a sudden, I knew I was no longer worried about the outcome of her life. I knew God had His hand upon her and she would indeed fulfill the call of God on her life. Thank God!

God cares about our problems even if we can't always explain them, and even if we can't identify them to Him. He knows what we are going through, and we can depend on Him to take care of the situation! Several weeks before I delivered, my friends and family gave me a wonderful little girl baby shower. At that time the only little girl outfit I had for the baby was one Lindsay had crocheted for her, and it was so precious.

I had dreamed just a few nights before the shower that after I had delivered the baby, I didn't have any clothes I could put her in to bring her home except that one tiny outfit. My new little girl was so big when she came to earth, that outfit was too small for her! (Aren't we silly with our thoughts and dreams?)

The shower was such a blessing. I was able to relax when I realized I now had *lots* of outfits for our new little girl no matter what her size. I went to the shower with my one little crocheted outfit and came back home with fifty-two of the most wonderful and gorgeous outfits — everything from sleepers to frilly pageant dresses in every size from newborn to two years old!

In the last week of May I began having contractions on and off for several hours at a time. One Sunday they started about 2:00 a.m. and continued regularly about five minutes apart. In the morning I called Dr. Mike to discuss the situation. He said for me to drink plenty of water because of dehydration and call him back in an hour. I drank the water and the contractions stopped.

I went to the doctor because a regular appointment was scheduled. Harry had taken me to every appointment, but today he was so busy trying to get everything ready for the baby to come that I convinced him to let his mother, Patricia, take me. I was not able to drive during any of this time, and she was such a help to me through the entire pregnancy.

As we returned home, I asked her to stay for lunch. I went in the house to fix us a bite while she went to the yard to play with the boys. The next thing I knew, Tracey's mom who was visiting, came running in the house to tell me Lil' Harry had knocked Patricia down when he was roller blading and she thought that she might have broken her collar bone.

Although I was supposed to be taking it easy, I figured it was time for the baby to be here anyway, so off to the doctor we went! I wasn't about to let anyone else take care of Patricia after all she had done for me. Sure enough, her collar bone was broken. After it was set, I drove her home.

I took care of her all day, trying to repay her just a little for all she had done for me over the years. Patricia had never been sick nor needed anyone to take care of her before, and I wanted to do something nice for her if at all possible. By evening I was exhausted and all of the family, especially Harry, convinced me to go home and get some rest.

By Tuesday I was pretty wiped out. I hadn't slept well Monday night because I was just too tired. Tuesday night came and I fell into bed exhausted. On Wednesday at 2:00 a.m. I woke up from a sound sleep having contractions strong enough to get me out of bed. I grabbed Benny Hinn's book, *Good Morning, Holy Spirit,* and my stop watch and went downstairs to the family room. I sat on the couch timing my contractions and reading until 7:00 a.m. Wednesday morning.

I called Denise and updated her on what had been happening during the night. She said it sounded like the real thing to her and advised me to call Dr. Mike. At eight o'clock I did just that. The doctor said things sounded serious, and if the contractions persisted until ten o'clock I should come to his office. I talked it over with Harry before he went to work, and he said he would come back to get me later.

By ten, the contractions were still rolling, so I dressed the boys and myself to go to the doctor. Harry came and picked us up. We wanted to be excited, but we thought this might be a false alarm. The doctor examined me and confirmed that I really was in labor. I could hardly believe it because I had felt no pain. I mean it. I had real contractions but no pain, so I was sure it must not be the real thing. I was dilated to four centimeters, and the doctor told us to head to the hospital.

We had the children with us, so we got them something to eat before heading back home. When we got home we grabbed the suitcase and went to the hospital. We weren't in any hurry, because we had done this twice before. Speed had never been my "thing" in childbirth, so there didn't seem to be any reason to get in a big rush.

We checked into the hospital around noon, but didn't even call our families or friends, since there didn't seem to be any hurry. I wasn't hurting at all, and I thought things would have to get a lot more intense before anything would happen. By 1:00 p.m. I was up to seven centimeters. Denise and Lindsay were both there with Harry and me by this time, and no one could believe there was no pain. I was sitting up cross-legged on the bed. The contractions were long and strong, but still there was no pain! It was a miracle.

You see, during the night as I read Benny Hinn's book on the Holy Spirit, I had discovered a great truth, one I had not known before. I had the Holy Spirit in my life and He was definitely active. But I had not realized the importance of welcoming Him into my *every* circumstance.

Now in labor, I used every contraction as my focal point to welcome the Holy Spirit. As each contraction began I said out loud, "Welcome, Holy Spirit, into this experience," and He would come. It was astounding to me that He would come into this delivery with such force.

By 2:00 p.m. there was still no pain, but there was a change. The contractions weren't as effective as before. Almost an hour passed, and Dr. Mike said this could go on for a long time. So he ordered a megadose of Pitocin drip to intensify the contractions. For the next ten minutes the contractions came one on top of the other. I have to admit these were not pleasant. In fact, these hurt very badly! But praise God, it only took ten minutes for my cervix to open up to the position needed to push.

By 3:20 p.m. I was ready to push, and push I did. Within just a few minutes and a few pushes Denise and Dr. Mike said they could see the baby's head. I didn't believe them and said, "Sure, you can!" I thought they were messing with my mind. I had never had a baby with so few pushes. But nine minutes and seven pushes later I had delivered the most beautiful baby you have ever seen.

Dr. Mike said, "It's a girl," and began to cry. I began to cry. Harry began to cry. We all began to cry. The anointing was so strong! Satan had fought so hard to keep her from getting here. We were all praising God together that she was finally here and it was over! Harry took one look at her and said, "You're going to break my heart." I knew then he was going to have the hardest time some day giving her away in marriage.

It's amazing how our lives connect the past, the present, and the future. I looked at this beautiful baby girl and felt the healing of the Lord rush all over me. I felt an absolute confirmation that God was going to use our little girl for His glory. She brought healing and complete restoration from my past hurts straight from heaven. I was finally free. The final layers of my healing were completed, and I could take one more step toward becoming the completed woman God created me to be.

Harry and I named her Gabrielle Christian Salem, which means "God's Christ-like messenger of peace." She was already fulfilling the prophecy of her name. There was pure peace over the delivery, over our hospital room, and over Harry and me.

God completed our family when He sent us Gabrielle, and He completed my healing from all the hurt and fear I had hidden deep inside all those years.

6
Don't Give Up!

I have decided that Satan is rather stupid, because he never seems to know when he is defeated and just keeps coming back for more punishment and defeat. As children of God, we must never get weary in our well doing. If we do then the ole' devil has a chance to get a lick in on us.

Harry and I had the chance to quit many times during my pregnancy with Gabrielle. Satan just wouldn't leave us alone, and we were tired of fighting. When we finally got her here, we thought we had won the battle and he would back off, but he didn't.

When Gabrielle was just a few weeks old we noticed she was having a problem with her breathing. In the night and sometimes in the day she would just quit breathing. She would take a big hard breath, then not take another one. At first we didn't recognize this as an attack of Satan, but it only took a short time to discover this was another one of his lies.

We took all the necessary precautions: doctors, tests, sleep monitors, etc. What an emotional roller coaster we were on! One night I was getting her ready for bed. I had bathed her, strapped on the sleep monitor, turned it on, and laid her in the infant carrier that she slept in right next to me. I was watching the news on television as a reporter came on. He reported that a baby had just been electrocuted by a sleep monitor minutes before!

I couldn't believe it! A few weeks previously I had never even heard of monitors to watch whether a baby is breathing or not, a condition called sleep apnea. Now I was sitting in front of my television with my baby beside me hooked up to a monitor, the same kind of monitor that had just killed the baby on the news!

I was frantic. I prayed about two minutes, then called Harry to come and pray with me as to what to do. We decided that our faith was with God and that we knew He would heal our daughter completely. Finally, after taking authority over the devil repeatedly, we were both in agreement that Satan was completely defeated. We unhooked her from that monitor that very night. She never had another attack nor even a sign of one!

Watching that news report was frightening, but it was the kick in the spiritual pants that Harry and I needed to proclaim liberty in our house concerning the healing of our baby. You have to stand your ground and not give Satan an inch. You can't let up. (Ephesians 6:10-18).

The devil is counting on us to get tired and give up. You have to remember what the Bible says about warfare in Ephesians. Read the verses out loud to yourself. Let your own ears hear you say, **And having done all, to stand. Stand therefore, having your loins girt about with truth** (Ephesians 6:13,14).

What does this mean to you? It should mean that no matter what Satan comes up with, God has commanded you to stand — not sit down, lie down, or quit — but stand!

This is a simple instruction for winning. It is called tenacity in your faith. It means you will hold on, no matter what it looks like. To do this, you gird your loins with truth, not facts. This is where so many well-meaning Christians miss it. They hear the facts spoken by the world, by the reporters, by the doctors, by circumstances and situations, and they gird their loins with facts. This is the surest way I know of to fail and quit.

God does not say for us to base our faith on the facts. He says to base our faith on the truth. God's truth is His Word, and God's Word does not always coincide with the facts — but our faith in God's Word can change the facts!

The doctors told us *facts* about Gabrielle. We could have based our faith on these facts. Instead we chose to base our faith on what God's Word says about healing. We chose to believe the truth and let God change the facts!

Facts can kill you. Facts can take your hope and faith. But truth, God's truth, will always set you free!

I don't know about you, but I am tired of being run around by the nose where Satan is concerned. He doesn't have a right to my life, to my family or to my ministry. He doesn't have any rights to anything!

I am taking back what God has given me. I choose once again to believe God instead of the circumstances that surround my life. This is a good time for you to stand up and declare to the devil that he is a loser and you are the winner. Proclaim out loud the promises of God. (Start reading 1 John 4:4, Psalm 91 and Isaiah 54:17 out loud to the devil.)

There are so many promises in God's Word for you. You will be amazed how many positive scriptures you will find in the Bible that apply to you and the very situation you are going through right now. God knows what you are going through, and He can and will deliver you out of it. But you need to stand your ground against the enemy and proclaim your freedom by God's Word!

7

It's Not Over Till You've Won!

We defeated Satan from destroying Gabrielle while she was still in the womb. Then she was healed from sleep apnea. You would think that was enough, that it was time for smooth sailing. That's certainly what I thought! I was fed up with battle after battle, war after war, wound after wound! A bright new day must be just around the bend, right?

WRONG! Gabrielle was fine, but Mommy was anything but fine. Mommy felt like her whole life was over. Or at least she wished that it could be!

I just couldn't seem to get it together. It was from so many things, and from nothing. Everything bothered me and nothing bothered me. Everything in me hurt and nothing in me hurt. Each day was a new challenge just to get from the beginning to the end.

I would get out of bed each day just barely able to put one foot in front of the other. I couldn't even make a decision as to what to put in the boy's lunch boxes for school. I felt lost, confused, buried underneath a million things and under nothing at all!

Do I sound like a complete basket case?! I was, and I didn't have a clue as to how to fix myself. I would lay on my face before the Lord day after day and say, "Stop the world, God. I want to get off." And, honestly, I really meant it. I began to lose my voice. I couldn't sing. I couldn't speak. I was nauseated all the time. I had violent headaches to the point that any light at all would make me want to throw up.

I was losing weight daily — and I didn't have any excess weight in the first place!

I can't tell you the desperation that I felt. I would have these long debates with myself. One side said, "Surely, you must be kidding, Cheryl! You have everything anyone could ever want! A wonderful husband, beautiful children, a comfortable home, a loving family, a full-time ministry!"

The other side of me just wanted to go on home and be with Jesus.

My mind and my body were under a complete onslaught from the enemy. It came so fast and so furiously that I didn't even have time to put up my defenses. By the time I realized some of what could be happening to me, I was too embarrassed to ask anyone to pray for me. Besides, I couldn't put my feelings into words. How could I ask for prayer? I didn't know what to ask for!

"God's people don't have a problem with their mind! God's people don't need help with depression!" This is what I would tell myself over and over! And I thought it was especially true for people like me, people who preached that a person could choose to be happy. I had done that for over ten years!

This couldn't be happening. I cried all the time — in private, in public, it didn't matter. It got so bad that I didn't want to leave the house for any reason. I just couldn't face the thought that someone might figure out what I was going through.

I know this sounds crazy! I guess that's what happens when Satan begins to attack your mind. I felt like I was in a maze. When I prayed I could see the way out. But standing in the maze, I couldn't find the exit out!

We went home for Christmas and my sister Paulette started in on me. She and I had been talking regularly on the phone, and she had already discerned that something was terribly wrong with me. But by the time she saw me I was almost a walking zombie. I couldn't sleep at all. I couldn't eat at all. I just made it through each day. Nothing more.

Paulette told me I had every classic symptom of chronic depression. I didn't want to hear this. My doctor had already told me this when I went to see him about my voice. I didn't want to believe him, and I didn't want to believe her either! She talked to me and talked to me, and wouldn't leave me alone. I got so mad at her I finally convinced Harry to pack us up and take us back home to Tulsa.

Even though my sister didn't know it, she had gotten my attention. All the way home (ten hours in a car) I thought about what she had said. I began to ask the Lord if she was right.

Of course, when you ask the Lord something, He is going to tell you the truth. He began to show me that what the doctor had been telling me and what my sister was telling me was the truth. The Father God began to reveal to me that He couldn't heal me if I wouldn't admit that I needed healing.

Lovingly, the Holy Spirit showed me that if I had a cold or a fever I would have no problem telling God what was the matter, and I would run to Him for my healing. If my leg were broken, I would ask for healing. The present problem, which happened to be a chemical imbalance in my brain, was also a physical problem that needed to be healed.

It's amazing how we can put ourselves into bondage because of preconceived notions instead of listening to the voice of the Holy Spirit when He talks to us. But I finally admitted to the Father that I needed His help and His healing, and God sent several other people to help me.

Lindsay brought me such comfort and enlightenment through the Word. Others brought prayers of support when I didn't even know what to ask for or even how to pray.

Months passed and I began to get discouraged. I wanted to be well. I wanted my singing voice and speaking voice back! I was beginning to get a little impatient with the whole thing. It seemed no matter what I did, more prayer, more commitment, more medicine, less work, less stress, nothing helped.

I went from one specialist to another trying to find someone who could help me with the real problem, not just mask the symptoms with a lot of medication. I was diagnosed with chronic depression, chronic fatigue syndrome, fibromialgia, connective tissue disease. You name it and I was told that I had it!

I got so tired trying to find out what was wrong that I finally said, "God, no matter what it is that is wrong, no matter what the root cause or the outward symptoms are, I believe I am getting better. I know that I am." This choice took me to a new plateau in my faith, but nothing changed on the outside. I was still very sick and extremely weak and fatigued.

Finally, I said to the Father God, "Nothing is working and I want to get well." The Father said to me, "Do what you know to do." *You must be kidding, God. I am doing what I know to do and it is not working!*

He said it to me again, "Do what you know to do."

Okay! I began to get out my old Bibles, the ones with the margins all written on, and began to read the verses out loud to myself. The more I read the happier I felt. The more I read the better I felt. Even if the feeling didn't last very long, at least it was a reprieve from the constant feelings of exhaustion. The more I read, the more God's Word began to get into my spirit and get me "out of my mind" so to speak!

This happened months after I first had the problems with the chemical imbalance, but it was the beginning of the healing. I wasn't well but I was on my way to being well! I was walking out my healing!

I continued to preach and teach to myself over the next coming months. A day finally came when I knew that I was ready to make a quality decision. It was more than just a mental choice. It was more than just a spiritual choice. It was an overall decision of my entire being that I was going to get better. From that day forth I knew that I knew that I was getting better. In fact, it was more than getting better. I was better!

Every day I was better than the day before. My strength began to come back. My weight started coming back up. My mind began to relax enough that I could sleep at night. I was getting better and there was nothing Satan could do about it!

This attack of the enemy had come upon me before I knew it. But God was faithful through the fire, and I am walking out on the other side now. I have had to make difficult decisions that I have not enjoyed, like staying at home and canceling more traveling dates. But God has been faithful to the call on my life and has allowed me to minister here in Tulsa like never before.

Depression. What an ugly word. I hate it. I hate admitting to anyone that I have had to fight depression, but it's the truth. But the greatest part of the entire fight is that I am winning against it. Thank God for spirit-filled doctors who will listen to the voice of the Holy Spirit and help you get better.

Depression really can be defeated. You don't have to learn to live with it. By using your faith, by the power of the Word of God, you really can rid your life of depression and be "normal" again. Sometimes it is a spirit of depression, sometimes it is a chemical imbalance, and sometimes it is both. We prayed, we got medical help, and we believed God to heal me. He did.

The most wonderful thing that I have learned from all of this is that depression is a sickness like any other sickness. If we don't admit that we have a problem then we can't get healed of that problem. But when we finally face the facts and admit the problem, God can move in on the scene and heal. And God can heal our brains, our minds, even our emotions. God can go past all of our fears, our preconceived notions, wherever the problem lies, and truly heal us. Praise God for His faithfulness!

Where was Harry through all of this? I should put Harry's picture next to the word "loyal" in my dictionary! He is always there for me: steady, reliable, faithful, and trustworthy.

Harry stayed by my side trying to help me find answers when I had the strength to look for them. And when I didn't have the strength, he searched on his own. He read everything he could get his hands on and talked to doctors, nurses, friends, whoever could shed light on this situation.

The best way I could describe myself through all of this is that I was lost somewhere, but I didn't know where. I just was not myself. And when I began to get better, I knew it. I began to say, "I feel like myself today."

What a wonderful feeling to know you have found something you have lost — especially if that something turns out to be you!

8
Restoration and Completion

There were times when I thought my life was what Joseph's life must have been like. (See Genesis, Chapters 37 to 45.) Everything looked like it was against me. Everything looked like it was taking me in the opposite direction of the fulfillment of my dream. But at that very time all of the trials and tribulations were taking me right into the completed and fulfilled promises of God.

As I look back on my life, especially the last few years of starting my family, I realize how hard Satan fought me. He did not want me to have a generation of children to whom I could pass the anointing of God. He wanted to stop God's promises in this generation. But he couldn't! He cannot defeat me, **because greater is He who is in me than he who is in the world** (1 John 4:4)! All of the situations and circumstances I have gone through were taking me to the completion of who I am called to be.

I began to realize the importance of a scripture I had meditated on for years. Psalms 37:4 says, **Delight yourself in the Lord, and He will give you the desires of your heart.** For several years I have taught, based on this scripture, that you have a choice. You can "choose to be happy."

This is true. But there is so much more to the decision than making a "head" choice to be happy. I am discovering every day that the Lord wants more of me than just my head choices. He wants me to get before Him and do what all of Psalm 37 says. He wants me to stop fretting and worrying, and to trust Him. Trust Him! Trust Him!

Are you understanding what I am saying? If you get yourself into a position to trust the Father God, then you can relax in Him and allow Him to transform your very character. He will give you perfect peace if you will quit focusing on your problems.

Stop worrying about whether somebody will think you are weird or not. Let God completely overtake you and you will get delighted in Him. You will get drunk on the new wine of the Holy Spirit (Acts, Chapter 2). You will forget all your troubles.

You might be saying, "Cheryl, that sounds good, but nothing could make me forget all my troubles." God can! He really can.

I am not saying you can't recall your problems when you try to remember them. But when you remember your troubles, they won't have the same weight they did before, because you are completely trusting God to take care of you and all your circumstances.

There is more to it than just a decision to give it all to Him. It starts with a decision, then it is followed with a complete yielding to the Holy Spirit. That means you trust God completely when the Holy Spirit moves upon you. The Holy Spirit is a gentleman, and He won't do anything in your life unless you give Him an open door. It all comes down to trust.

Do you trust God enough to yield your entire being to Him — body, soul (mind, emotions) and spirit? When you choose to trust Him completely, that's when you can literally become drunk in the Spirit of God. You won't care what people say. You won't care if you are a fool for Christ. You won't care how long it takes for all of your needs to be met. You relax in Him and rest in Him, because you are experiencing sheer joy — **the perfect peace of one whose mind is stayed on Thee** (Isaiah 26:3).

You see, the world turns to alcohol to experience a temporary escape from their problems. Any "peace" that comes from drinking is a counterfeit to God's rest and peace. This "solution" offered by the world has many drawbacks, everything from a hangover to the realization that there is no lasting peace when it is all over. However, when we have given ourselves completely over to God and the Holy Spirit, there are no side effects, no hangovers, and no drawbacks. There is nothing like it in the whole world.

I have only recently experienced this complete surrendering of myself to God in this way. I grew up in a precious little Methodist church in Choctaw County, Mississippi. I learned much about God's love and what Jesus has done for me. I received Christ as my Lord and Savior in that church. But the Holy Spirit was not presented to us there. (We had a duet in our church, not a trio!)

As I grew up in the Lord and received the Holy Spirit in my life (in a Kenneth Hagin meeting), I discovered a whole new realm of walking with God. There was only one problem. I had never gotten over my conservative roots when it came to worshipping the Lord.

Those of you who know me are probably saying, "You must be kidding! You think you are *conservative*!" The truth is, I am very free with my praise and even with my worship, but not with myself! I couldn't give God all of my life. I could praise Him, I could give my testimony in any situation regardless of how uncomfortable that situation might be. But to give my whole being, my body, soul, mind, and spirit, was just a little too much for me. Especially in public.

What if I made a fool of myself? What if He asked me to dance or shout or RUN for His glory? Heaven forbid! The one thing I always asked God from the beginning of my ministry was, "Please God, don't make me be weird!"

Aren't we silly? We say to the Father, "Take me, use me whatever way You want, but please don't do it in a way that might embarrass me in front of the world!" Isn't that ridiculous? God does not make us weird. But He does tell us that when we belong to Him we will be a peculiar people (1 Peter 2:9).

Webster's Dictionary (2nd College edition) definition of peculiar is "of only one person, thing, group, country, etc.; distinctive; exclusive; particular; unique; special, something belonging to one only as a privilege." God's Word tells us we are set apart, that we are holy unto God. (See Exodus 19:5; Deuteronomy 14:2, 26:18; Psalm 135:4; Titus 2:14). We may seem different from the world, but that's because we are different. We belong to God, and He has made us uniquely His own.

I love the way Titus 2:14 (AMP) reads:

> **Who gave Himself on our behalf that He might redeem us (purchase our freedom) from all iniquity and purify for Himself a people—to be peculiarly His own —[people who are] eager and enthusiastic about [living a life that is good and filled with] beneficial deeds.**

The next verse helped me to understand that God did not expect me to become the world's laughing stock just because I belong to Him. Titus 2:15 (AMP) says:

> **Tell [them all] these things. Urge (advise, encourage, warn) and rebuke with full authority. Let no one despise or disregard or think little of you—conduct yourself and your teaching so as to command respect.**

God is telling us to use the authority that He has given us. We are to look like we belong to God, talk like we belong to God, and walk like we belong to God. Why? Because we DO belong to God and have been given full authority through His Word (Genesis 1:26,27). God does not expect us to be anyone's laughing stock, but He does expect us to be His peculiar people, set apart and holy for His glory.

In the privacy of my home I could "get down" worshipping the Lord with the best of them. To dance before the Lord, shout out purest praise, or whatever I wanted to do was just fine at home. But to be expected to do this in a worship service with other people present just wasn't me. Or so I thought.

God wants all of us, even the deepest recesses of our being. One thing about our Father, if you present yourself to him as a yielded vessel, He will do what He needs to do to completely free you before Him.

It's not the same for everyone. In my case, I had to give into my pride and become a "fool" for Christ. I use the word "fool" carefully because from what I have experienced there are enough fruits and nuts in the body of Christ to open a granola factory. But there is a difference in being a "plain ole' fool" and being a "fool for Christ."

The "fool for Christ" is the person who is willing to risk it all, to completely let down all his barriers and trust God even to the point of getting "beside himself." This is what God is looking for. I want to be that person. That means I can't worry about appearance or how I present myself to the people around me when I worship my Father God.

You see, it is not a certain outward action God is looking for, but the motive of your heart is what He sees. If we are worrying (because of pride) what others will think of us instead of becoming completely vulnerable to the Father God and experiencing an intimate relationship with Him, our pride will stop God's best from happening in our lives!

I have finally gotten to the point where I can completely trust God and "let my spiritual hair down." It took a spiritual "drunken" experience for me to get to that point. Now I know firsthand what truly delighting myself IN THE LORD really means. First, I choose to be happy with my head. Second, I allow the Holy Spirit to overtake me. I get so completely wrapped up in Him that I act, look, and feel like they must have on the day of Pentecost described in the second chapter of Acts. There, the onlookers thought the entire crowd was drunk on wine.

I don't know what it feels like to be drunk on earthly wine, but I do know what it feels like to be drunk on the heavenly wine of the Holy Spirit. And I wouldn't trade the freedom I experience for anything in the whole world. Try it. You'll like it!

After having Gabrielle, the anointing on my life and ministry has exploded. I am so thankful to the Father for this fresh outpouring of "new wine" into my life.

Each phase of my life has taken me into a different dimension of God and His power. But nothing has brought about the growth in my spiritual life like our four children. Lil' Harry brought me strength. Roman brought me joy. Malachi brought me compassion. Gabrielle brought me healing. Strength, joy, compassion and healing were all vital to my personal growth and to my ministry.

My precious husband, Harry, has lived with me for these past years and walked with me through all of these emotional valleys. Through Harry's patience, covering, and training I am finally becoming more of the woman God has called me to be. I guess I will still be "becoming" that woman when the Lord comes back to take us home with Him. But it certainly is nice to be able to look back over my life and see some maturity evolving from the struggles.

We are not automatically equipped with the ability to parent when we have our first child. We probably don't learn how to be a really good parent until we become grandparents. Maybe that's why my mom says, "I wasn't a very good mother, but I am a great grandmother!"

Mom, you were a great mother as far as I am concerned, but I finally understand why you would say that. We certainly learn as we go along, don't we?

One thing about it, though. Our relationship with the Father God should improve after we become parents. That is because we begin to understand what He has been going through with us from the beginning.

God is the most patient teacher, and I am sure it is His will for us to be the best parents on the earth. We need to learn to listen to His voice, follow His lead, and relax. Our children will be the better for it.

I have prayed more prayers for forgiveness as a parent than ever before in my life. I am positive I have asked my children to forgive me more for my mistakes in rearing them than any other human on the face of the earth!

Regularly I explain to Lil' Harry that Mommy is learning to be a good mommy just like he is learning to be a good son. This helps him to forgive me and also makes him realize that parents aren't perfect.

I think it's good for children to hear their parents ask God for forgiveness. Then they can understand that all people, even parents, make mistakes. But we have an advocate with our heavenly Father. God is waiting with open arms to forgive us and take us back on His lap for a little loving time (1 John 1:9). I thank God that we have a right to run to Him at all times.

You might want to pray this prayer with me now:

"Father God, thank You for loving me when I wasn't very lovely. Thank You for sending Your Son, Jesus, to die on the cross for my sins so I could be back in Your arms again. Thank You for trusting me enough to rear these precious children in the admonition of the Lord.

"Every day they are anointed in the Name of the Father, the Son, and the Holy Spirit (2 Timothy 2:19, Exodus 28:41, 29:7). I plead the blood of Jesus over them, under them, and all around them (Hebrews 10:19, 1 Peter 1:2, 1 John 1:7). I ask You, Father, in Jesus name, to appoint four angels around my children on every side to guard, guide, and protect them (Psalms 91:11,12; 34:7; Daniel 3:28, 6:22). I put a prayer cover over them and a wall of prayer around them (Psalms 91:4).

"All my children shall be taught of the Lord and great shall be their peace and undisturbed composure (Isaiah 54:13). Thank You, Father, for putting Your hand on my children and calling them into Your service (Mark 16:17, Philippians 3:14).

"In the mighty Name of Jesus! Amen! Hallelujah!"

Every day I pray this prayer. I believe God that His Word is true. It is full of power. Not one word of His Word will return void (Isaiah 54:11).

In all of my learning and growing, I have discovered that I will never fully arrive. The strength, joy, compassion, and healing that my children have brought into my life is an on-going growing process. This means that I must allow God to deal with my weaknesses as well as use my strengths, and that I trust Him to complete what He has started in me.

Learning to be a parent has taught me how to be a child — a child of the King, that is.

My four children are my great blessings:

Lil' Harry — STRENGTH,

Roman — JOY,

Malachi — COMPASSION, and

Gabrielle — HEALING.

Strength, joy, compassion, healing: all four of these character-building qualities are transforming me into more of what I am called to be. As I strive for perfection in Christ Jesus, it causes more strength, joy, compassion, and healing to be activated in my life, and then I can pour these things into others!

Before I married Harry and we had our children, I thought I was comfortable, confident, and seasoned at being a child of the King. But after I became a parent, I have seen repeatedly how little I knew about being a child of God! In this growing, changing process, I am learning how to be a strong child, a joyful child, a compassionate child, and a healed child.

I am learning how to be A ROYAL CHILD!

Order Form —
Cheryl Salem Library

If you would like more teaching materials or if you have a friend or loved one who needs help in a certain area of his or her life, just write for some of these materials.

Books	Price	Quantity
You Are Somebody	$5.95	_____

    (This is great for those who have
    developed a poor self-image
    due to many different reasons.)

A Bright-Shining Place	$6.95	_____

    (This is Cheryl's life story of how
    God raised her from a crippled little
    girl in Choctaw County, Mississippi,
    to Miss America in 1980. It will show
    you what making the right choices
    can do for you!)

ABUSE: Bruised but Not Broken!	$2.95	_____

    (Abuse of all kinds — physical, mental,
    emotional — is found in many homes.
    This book can help the abused and the
    abuser work through their past and
    live a productive life with a good self-image.)

How To Get a . . . BALANCED BODY!	$3.95	_____

    (A "show-and-tell" book of how to
    reduce those troublesome spots and
    bring your body into perfect balance
    by eating a balance of healthy,
    nourishing foods — in moderation.)

Royal Child $5.99 _____
   (Cheryl's autobiography, beginning
   with her marriage to Harry Salem,
   their life together, their ministry and
   their children.)

The Mommy Book $8.99 _____
   (A 31-day devotional for frazzled
   moms with busy children.)

Mini-books

Health and Beauty Secrets $ .75 _____
   (The tips Cheryl shares in this little
    book are very practical in answering
   questions concerning health and
   beauty. They can help you become
   the best YOU that you can be!)

Choose To Be Happy $ .75 _____
   (This book is small, but powerful.
   It holds the secret to being happy
   all the time. It's great for people in
   all walks of life.)

*Simple Facts: Salvation, Healing
and the Holy Ghost* $ .75 _____
   (This book gives you the steps to
   take once you've been saved,
   baptized with the Holy Spirit
   [speaking in tongues], or healed,
   to make sure you develop the
   way God wants you to.)

Music Projects

Choose to be Happy Cassette $7.95 _____
   (All-music cassette
   with happy songs)

Ain't Nothin' Gonna Stop   Cassette $7.95   _____
You Now
    (Motivational music)

The Music and Ministry of Cheryl   Cassette $7.95   _____
    (Miraculous testimony of Cheryl's
    healing, the story of winning
    Miss America, plus four songs.)

Living Proof   Cassette $7.95   _____
    (All-music cassette from
    "Richard Roberts Live" telecast,
    including: "Devil, Pick on
    Somebody Your Own Size,"
    "I'm Not Lettin' Myself Get
    Down," and many more.)

With All my Heart   Cassette $7.95   _____
    (Inspirational tracks including:
    "You Are Somebody," "I Will Not
    Be Afraid," and "Don't Give In.")

My Heritage   Cassette $7.95   _____
    (Old favorites like "How Great
    Thou Art," and "Jesus Lord to Me/
    I Exalt Thee.")

Makin' My Dreams Come True Cassette $9.95   _____
    (Upbeat and new, this recording
    comes from the heart with songs,
    "It's Too Soon," and title track,
    "Making My Dreams Come True.")

Audio Teaching Tapes

ABUSE: Bruised but Not Broken! $4.00   _____
    (You will feel the healing anointing in
    this single audio cassette in which Cheryl
    deals directly with emotions and self-image
    that are a direct result of abuse of every kind.)

Angels I and II $4.00   _____
    (An awe-inspiring, two-tape series,
    based on Cheryl's own experiences
    with heavenly beings.)

Breaking the Curse $4.00   _____
    (Healing generational curses)

Choices $4.00   _____
    (Traveling the right path by
    following His will through life's
    difficult decisions)

Courage $4.00   _____
    (In today's society it takes more
    than just "want to" to accomplish
    what God has called us to do —
    thus this teaching tape on courage.)

Depression $4.00   _____
    (Overcoming the low points, moving
    on to a healthy and happy lifestyle)

Fear $4.00   _____
    (How to overcome affliction in
    your thoughts.)

God's Principles to Prosper You $4.00   _____
    (The importance of sacrifice in
    all areas)

Your Inheritance $4.00   _____
    (How to pray more effectively for
    God's will in your life.)

How To Know the Will of God $4.00   _____
    (Scripture-based teaching on
    following His path for you.)

How to Get Healed $4.00 _____
    (God's best for you through His
    healing power.)

Male and Female, What a Difference $4.00 _____
    (Simple differences that really matter.)

Nutrition $4.00 _____
    (This single audio cassette is a must
    for everyone who has bought the
    Balanced Body book. Cheryl adds
    insights that will be a great addition
    to what you learn from this book.)

Proverbs 31 Woman $4.00 _____
    (A single cassette teaching you God's
    beautiful description of what a woman
    can become at her best.)

Rest: Ahh, Peace and Quiet $4.00 _____
    (Learn the importance of taking
    time out to be with the Lord.)

Self-Image I and II $6.00 _____
    (This wonderful two-tape set
    provides you with a feeling of
    worthiness in being a child of God.)

Submission and Obedience $4.00 _____
    (Scriptural guidance for becoming
    a true servant)

The Anointing $4.00 _____
    (How to become tuned-in and
    carry this special touch from
    the Holy Ghost.)

The Unstoppable Dream $4.00 _____
    (The story of Joseph as a
    parallel of your dreams.)

Thought Life: Crucified or Uncrucified? $4.00 _____
    (How to have a healthy and
    productive mindset.)

Aerobic Video Tapes

Take Charge of Your Life $15.00 (special _____
with Cheryl and Friends   Usually $19.95
    (High-impact aerobics video)

Get Ready with Cheryl and Friends $15.00 (special) _____
    (Low-impact aerobics video)   Usually $19.95

Cheryl's Defense Video $15.00 (special) _____
    (Nine self-defense moves   Usually $19.95
    incorporated into aerobics)

Teaching Video Tapes

Depression $14.95 _____
    (Overcoming the low points
    and moving on to a healthy
    and happy lifestyle)

Desperate Situations Require $14.95 _____
Daring Faith
    (Video coverage of Cheryl on
    concentrating on your beliefs
    to get through the circumstances)

God's Principles to Prosper You $14.95 _____
    (Video coverage of Cheryl on the
    importance of sacrifice in all areas)

Your Inheritance $14.95_____
(Video coverage of Cheryl
speaking in Edmonton, Canada,
on understanding how to pray more
effectively for God's will in your life.)

Magnificent Joy $14.95_____
(Video coverage of Cheryl in
Edmonton, Canada. Watch the
joy explode!)

Male and Female, What a Difference $14.95_____
(This hilarious video shows the
simple differences that really matter)

Rest: Ahh, Peace and Quiet $14.95_____
(Watch and learn the importance of
taking time out to be with the Lord.)

Your Are Somebody $14.95_____
(This wonderful video provides
you with a feeling of worthiness
in being a child of God)

The Unstoppable Dream $14.95_____
(The story of Joseph as a parallel
of your dreams.)

Thought Life: Crucified or Uncrucified? $14.95_____
(In this video Cheryl covers how
to have a healthy and productive
mindset)

TOTAL AMOUNT ENCLOSED $_____

Just clip this order form and mail with
your check or money order to:

Cheryl Salem
P.O. Box 701287
Tulsa, OK 74170

If you have any questions or comments, just write to
the address above or call (918) 298-0770. Please feel free
to include your prayer requests. Please print:

Name_____

Address_____

City _____ State _____ Zip _____

Phone Number _____